Cittaviveka
Teachings from the silent mind.

Venerable Ajahn Sumedho

A selection of Dhamma talks by Ven. Ajahn Sumedho
of Chithurst Forest Monastery, West Sussex, England;
with narratives of the monastic life.

FOR FREE DISTRIBUTION ONLY

DEDICATION

This book has been printed for free distribution through the generosity of Mrs. Vanee Lamsam in memory of her late husband, Mr. Khasem Lamsam, and her daughter, Vachareevan Lamsam.

May all beings live happily, free from fear, and may all share in the blessings springing from the good that has been done.

For free distribution.

Publications from Amaravati are for free distribution.
In most cases, this is made possible through offerings
from individuals or groups, given specifically for
the publication of Buddhist teachings.
    For further information, please contact the
Publications Secretary, Amaravati Buddhist Centre.

Sabbadānam dhammadānam jināti
    'The gift of Dhamma
    surpasses all other gifts.'

Several editions of *Cittaviveka: Teachings from the Silent Mind*
have been published since 1983. This edition was updated in 1987.
We wish to express our gratitude to Pamutto Donohoe, for his work
and generosity in preparing the cover and many of the photographs
for this edition.

Published by
Amaravati Publications
Amaravati Buddhist Centre
Great Gaddesden
Hemel Hempstead
Hertfordshire HP1 3BZ
England

ISBN   1 870205 02 2

Printed by Amarin Printing Group Co., Ltd.
413 / 27-36 Arun Amarin Rood
Bangkok Noi, Bangkok 10700, Thailand. 1988

CONTENTS

Entrance to Chithurst Buddhist Monastery *(Wat Pah Cittavivek)*

INTRODUCTION

'Cittaviveka', the title of this book, is a Pali term generally meaning 'detached mind'. As our attachments to impermanent conditions cause us suffering, the 'detached mind' is the aim of the Buddhist path. Yet it is only attachment that creates the impression of a substantial, permanent mind, and as long as that model is retained, our attempts to grasp at freedom, and conceive the unconditioned, can only give rise to further painful attachments. A 'detached mind' is not another conditioned thing, but a continual sensitive response that Ajahn Sumedho frequently calls 'letting go'. A teaching that gets past attachment has to work as a foil to our grasping nature: the paradoxical subtitle with its 'silent teachings' points to the reflective insight that arises through mindfulness, a teaching that cannot be known or transmitted, but only remembered. So the book is not a meditation manual - although meditation is an essential aspect of the Path it points out - but an offering for some wise reflection.

'Cittaviveka' is also a name (Wat Pah Cittavivek) coined as an aspiration, and slight word-play, for Chithurst Forest Monastery. It was interest centred on the monastery that caused the book to be composed. The monastery currently receives a lot of attention in Buddhist circles in Britain, due to the combination of the pastoral serenity of West Sussex, the presence of a growing 'Western' Sangha, and the simple approach to Theravada teaching offered by the Thai Forest tradition through Ven. Sumedho Bhikkhu. The contribution to the monastery that has been made in terms of spiritual resources by Ven. Ajahn Chah and material support by the people of Thailand cannot be exaggerated. This book then is a tribute to them.

Since its first appearance, 'Cittaviveka' has been reprinted twice because of its popularity, and because good-hearted people have continued to delight in making the teachings freely available in a written form. In 1987, the Sangha was approached by people interested in producing another reprint, and so with a few alterations to update the first chapter, this new edition is being prepared. May it prove to be for the welfare of many.

Venerable Sucitto
Amaravati Buddhist Centre
August 1987

A Note on the Text

A good deal of this material has been printed before. Chapters
II, III--2, IV, V-3, VII, VIII and X have appeared in **The Middle Way,**
the journal of the Buddhist Society of Great Britain, whose requests
for articles largely instigated the recording of talks. As the chapters
from Ajahn Sumedho are all from **talks,** they have required some editing
to put them into a book form, though the 'voice' is unmistakeable and
intrinsic to what he is saying. Different contexts, environment and
audience create different tones and standards of practice - as perhaps
Chapter II most clearly points out.

Chapters I and X were written as articles on request, the first
for the Hampshire Buddhist Society's **Journal** (summer 1982) and the
second for **The Middle Way.** Despite the imagined objectivity of narra-
tive, they are also 'talks' - perspectives from one person's (my) mind.
Chapter I is the accumulation and sifting of several people's accounts,
particularly Ajahn Sumedho, Ven. Anando, M. O'C. Walshe, G. Sharp,
and G. Beardsley.

Sucitto Bhikkhu
Chithurst Forest Monastery
May 1983

Chithurst Buddhist Monastery

The Shrine, Chithurst Forest Monastery

'Walk, bhikkhus, on tour for the blessing of the manyfolk, for the happiness of the manyfolk, out of compassion for the world, for the welfare, the blessing, the happiness of devas and men... Bhikkhus, teach dhamma which is lovely at the beginning, lovely in the middle, lovely at the ending.'

Mahāvagga I — 20

HOW THE BUDDHA CAME TO SUSSEX

In the summer of 1976, Ajahn Sumedho requested permission from his teacher, Ven. Ajahn Chah of Wat Pah Pong in North-East Thailand, to visit his aging parents in California. He had not seen them since leaving America in 1964, weary of the West and drawn by an interest in Chinese studies and Eastern religion to volunteer for service with the Peace Corps in Sabah, Borneo. World-weariness and an interest in Eastern religion have a way of breeding good bhikkhus, and it was not long before he became Sumedho Bhikkhu, living under the guidance of a meditation teacher, Ven. Ajahn Chah, in a forest monastery in Ubon Province, Thailand.*

Time flowed by with its own teaching: one who endured the hardships and trials of the *dhutanga* monasteries acquired inner strength and patience even without the sometimes aggravating, sometimes playful, and frequently awe-inspiring teaching methods of a master such as Ajahn Chah. The teaching was a whole training in 'letting go', in giving oneself up to the routines, the Vinaya (monastic discipline), the simple austerity of the requisites of food, clothing and shelter that were offered, and to the will of the teacher. Ajahn Chah, with compassion and notorious humour, would tease and frustrate his disciples out of

---

*   'Ajahn' is a Romanisation of a Thai word which derives from, and is equivalent to, the Pali word 'Ācariya' meaning teacher or guide. In monastic usage it implies authority, as junior bhikkhus are expected to train at least five years in obedience to their Ajahn. It is also commonly spelt "Achaan"
'dhutanga' = 'austere' (see Chap X)
'Rains' - the seniority of a bhikkhu (monk) is measured by the number of yearly monsoon retreat seasons that he has spent in the robes.

their self-conceit, and those who really wanted to be delivered from their selfishness, resignedly, and eventually with gratitude and devotion, placed themselves under his guidance for a minimum period of five years. After seven Rains, Sumedho was allowed to go off on his own, and he wandered in India for five months, keeping to the strict Vinaya training of *dhutanga* bhikkhus - no money, no storing of food, and one meal per day, to be eaten out of the alms bowl before noon. Somehow in India, living on faith, it worked, and the respect for the tradition that this instilled in Ven. Sumedho encouraged him to return to Ajahn Chah and offer himself up body and mind to serve his teacher. Ajahn Chah's response is not recorded-it was probably no more than a wry smile or a grunt - but in his eighth year, Ven. Sumedho was given the task of establishing a monastery for Western bhikkhus in a haunted forest a few kilometres from Pah Pong, known as Bung Wai.

Having made the necessary mistakes, he became the Ajahn of a monastery that has developed into something of a showpiece in the forest tradition. Thai people, local villagers at first, and subsequently more cosmopolitan folk from Bangkok, were impressed by the presence of Western bhikkhus who had given up the wealth, university education and conveniences of Europe and America to live a sweat-soaked life that was austere even by the rustic tastes of North-East Thailand. Accordingly the monastery, Wat Pah Nanachat (International Forest Monastery), was well-supported and acquired a wealth of sponsorship that far exceeded the expectations of its Ajahn. More important, within a couple of years the modest foundation of four bhikkhus swelled to a sizeable group of bhikkhus, samaneras, *por kaos* and *maichees**.

It was at this time, in his tenth year as a bhikkhu, that Ajahn Sumedho responded to his father's request by visiting his parents in America. He stopped off in London on his way back, and as the Thai temple in Wimbledon, Wat Buddhapadipa, was rather crowded, decided

---

*   Whereas a 'bhikkhu' is a fully ordained 'monk', 'samanera' is a novitiate stage, which in Thailand is often reserved for those too young for full ordination. 'Por kao' and 'maichee' are Eight Precept monastics, male and female respectively, that in England, we call anagarika and anagarikā.

to use the telephone number that had been given to him by Ven. Paññāvaddho Bhikkhu, and contact George Sharp, Chairman of the English Sangha Trust and thereby custodian of the empty Hampstead Buddhist Vihara. Ven. Paññāvaddho had been the Senior Incumbent of the Vihara between 1957 and 1962, having succeeded the founder of the Trust, Ven. Kapilavaddho. After an incumbency of five years, Ven. Paññāvaddho had felt an interest in deepening his practice by living in the traditional forest environment of meditating bhikkhus, and had gone to Thailand to live under the guidance of Ven. Ajahn Maha Boowa. Ajahn Maha Boowa, like Ajahn Chah, stressed the importance of meditation, Vinaya and simplicity of life style, and also had a very fine forest monastery in North-East Thailand.

The English Sangha Trust, the stewards and owners of the Vihara, had been established in 1956 with the express aim of providing a suitable residence for bhikkhus in England. By 1972, it was time to consider why this aim had not been achieved, and in some people's minds now seemed an impossibility. There were numerous views and opinions but largely the chairman was caused to consider the nature of the environment and the life-style of the bhikkhus. Several of the incumbents had been gifted Dhamma teachers, but none of them had experience of the traditional bhikkhu life, with its training conventions, and mendicant relationship with the laity. So Mr. Sharp had taken up correspondence with Ven. Paññāvaddho, who had taken up that very life style and obviously found it preferable to the 'progressive' atmosphere of Western Buddhism. In 1974, this correspondence had resulted in the Trust's invitation to Ven. Ajahn Maha Boowa and Ven. Paññāvaddho to visit Hampstead, where their presence was so inspiring that there was some hope that Ven. Paññāvaddho might remain in England, accompanied by other forest bhikkhus. After Ajahn Sumedho's visit in 1976, Mr. Sharp went out to North-East Thailand himself to visit the forest monasteries and make a further request to the two meditation teachers to send forest bhikkhus to England. Ven. Ajahn Maha Boowa, perhaps because he had visited the Hampstead Vihara and seen all the difficulties that lay ahead in a country where people were ignorant of the bhikkhus' discipline and the relationship between Sangha and laity, was rather doubtful of the idea. The Vihara, a town house opposite a pub on a main road in North London, didn't seem suited for forest monks. Ajahn Chah, however, decided to visit in 1977, and when he came he brought Ajahn Sumedho with him.

Perhaps it was just another of Ajahn Chah's tests to make his disciples 'let go', but as a result of the visit, he left Ajahn Sumedho at Hampstead with three other of his Western disciples, to stay until more suitable forest premises became available. The daily life was conducted in a manner that was based on the monastic routine of the forest monastery, with morning and evening chanting, a daily alms-round *(pindapada)* and instruction to lay visitors to the Vihara. It was not an easy time for the bhikkhus–apart from the culture shock and the sudden cramping of their environment there was a lot of confusion as to the role of the Vihara, and how the tradition was to be altered, if at all, to fit English conditions. Perhaps in this country it was not appropriate to live in forests at all. In this atmosphere of doubt, it was only the bhikkhus' training in endurance and obedience to the discipline and the structure of the Sangha that preserved a degree of harmony.

In the spring of 1978, one of those small miracles happened that stop the mind's rational expectations. Keeping to the apparently pointless routine of going out for alms every day, as prescribed by Ajahn Chah, Ajahn Sumedho encountered a lone jogger on Hampstead Heath whose attention was arrested by the bhikkhus' appearance. He had acquired an overgrown forest in West Sussex called Hammer Wood out of the wish to restore it to its former glory, but he also understood that this was work for more than one man and one lifetime. Although not a Buddhist, he had the openness of mind to appreciate that an order of forest monks might be the perfect wardens for his woodland. Subsequently he attended one of the ten-day meditation retreats that Ajahn Sumedho held at the Oaken Holt Buddhist Centre near Oxford, and later made an outright gift of the forest to the Sangha. This marvellous act of generosity did of necessity involve a lot of legalities as local bye laws prevented the construction of any permanent structures on forest land, so in this situation, the Sangha gratefully accepted the invitation to stay at Oaken Holt for the 'Rains' of 1978 and let the Trust sort things out.

Early in 1979 Ajahn Chah was invited to England to see how his disciples were making out, and George Sharp, hearing that a large house near Hammer Wood was coming up for sale, agreed to purchase it. This was Chithurst House, and its purchase was a gamble that did not meet with unanimous approval. Buying the property had necessitated selling the Vihara and the adjacent town house whose rent had provided the basis of support for the Sangha, in order to purchase an unsurveyed and ramshackle mansion. In May Ajahn Chah arrived, somewhat disturbed by rumours of his disciples' activities, to find a monastic community that actually had nowhere to live. The new owners allowed the Sangha to use the Vihara for a couple of months to receive the Ven. Ajahn and to effect our move. In this atmosphere of insecurity, Ajahn Chah added one more doubt by intimating that he was going to take Ajahn Sumedho back to Thailand. While we watched our minds, he went off to America for a visit and there was nothing else to do but go ahead. On 22nd. June 1979, having bundled as much as we could into a removal van, we left London for Sussex.

Chithurst House really was a mess. Small work parties sent down earlier had done some preliminary work on clearing the grounds, but they had been denied access to the main house. The owner had let the place run to seed: uncleared gutters had broken and spilled water over the walls so that dry rot had spread. As things had broken down they had been abandoned; when we moved in, only four of the twenty or so rooms were still in use. The electricity had blown, the roof leaked, the floors were rotten and there was only one cold water tap for washing. The house was full of junk: all kinds of bric-a-brac from pre-war days. The outhouses were crumbling, roofs stoved in by fallen trees. The cesspit had not been emptied for twenty-five years. The gardens were overgrown: a fine walled fruit garden was a chest-high sea of nettles. Over thirty abandoned cars protruded though the brambles that smothered the vicinity of the old coach-house. But as we started to scrape through the mess, it felt all right. The situation left no alternatives; for better or worse, opinion was polarised and those who disagreed left. We had the support of the Arama Fund - a trust established by Ven. Paññāvaddho to help found a monastery in the West - which purchased the lovely meadows around the house. So the omens were good.

A stir of publicity initiated by the BBC's "The Buddha Comes to Sussex" brought us a lot of attention - a mixed blessing, as this gave rise to the 'invasion fears' of a body of local opinion that proved awkward later. But at first it was enormous fun. The summer was fine, we had a steady influx of volunteer labour, and we all worked hard. We were loaned a marquee by a local Buddhist businessman which served as a kitchen and dining hall. The weeds and debris in the grounds were attacked, temporary showers installed, drainage cleared and work begun on the kitchen. The community for Vassa consisted of six bhikkhus, two samaneras, eight anagarikas, four women in training to become anagarikas and three or four lay people staying for various periods of time. It was a spiritual refuge that gradually took on a monastic form. In September the women were given a separate place to live when a beautiful little cottage adjacent to Hammer Wood was rented for their use. About a year after their ordination as anagarikas in October, it was purchased with an estate that actually forms the ecological heart of the forest. Also in October, our two samaneras were given *upasampada* by Ven. Dr Saddhātissa,* using the River Thames as a *sīma* boundary. So by the winter, we had a 'monastery' and a 'nunnery', and a sizeable group of bhikkhus going out for nonexistent alms every morning.

This spectacle must have been more alarming than we thought, and at first there was a lot of mis-trust and reserve in the minds of local people, who tended to bracket any Eastern religion in the category of cults of idol worshippers following strange - or even worse - *no* gods. The discipline with its emphasis on harmlessness and modesty again helped us out where no amount of teaching of Buddhist Philosophy would have done - our neighbouring farmer, for example, had been impressed that, although we were not going to kill the rabbits that live on our property and invaded his fields, we went to the trouble and expense of

---

upasampada = higher ordination. Ven. Dr. Saddhātissa, the senior Theravada bhikkhu in Britain, is the Senior Incumbent of the London Buddhist Vihara.

building a rabbit fence to keep them *in*. It was our effect on the environment and our neighbours that finally made the district council grant Chithurst House monastic status with the freedom to train bhikkhus and nuns and live the monastic life in its conventional way.

This permission came about in March 1981, by which time the monastery had established itself in other ways. In the summer of 1979 we constructed a kitchen and shivered through the winter wearing caps, scarves and woollen underwear until the wood–burning stove that was to heat the house arrived in March of 1980. Work continued throughout that year, during which time one half of the house was gutted from basement to top floor and its rotten floors, doors and window frames removed and burnt, so that we could create a new Shrine Room. The second winter called a halt to the work programme as available funds ran out. The monastery is totally dependent on donations, which tend to dry up in the winter. Ajahn Sumedho decided that this would be the perfect opportunity for a monastic retreat, and this is a pattern that has established itself as a splendid opportunity to have a yearly quiet period of intensive practice. At the end of the monastic retreat in February 1981, the Buddha finally came to Sussex in the form of a half–ton Buddha image sent by a generous lay Buddhist from Thailand. This was a cheering sign, work began with renewed vigour, and the evening before Asalha Puja began the Rains of 1981, the new Shrine Room, dominated by this radiant image, was finished.

For that Rains, at last, the community had a long break. Work had been the major practice at Chithurst. Despite a couple of brief retreats, by and large the preoccupations were technical and material, rather than scriptural or contemplative. Sometimes work would go on well into the night to complete a project. At one time the dam by the cottage showed signs of breaking up – so, whatever, it had to be fixed as quickly as possible. People would get exhausted and complain about not being able to meditate, but for the most part they understood that it was a trial period, a changing condition that, like any other, could afford insight into the Four Noble Truths once the situation was accepted. It was actually a very good time for practice: good Vinaya, good teaching, good support and a stable Sangha. One can even imagine that in the future people will be taking about the "good old days when the going was tough."

A *sima* (boundary), defining a consecrated area for ordinations and official Sangha functions, was established by Ven. Anandamaitreya on 3rd June 1981 in the grounds where (currently in a teepee!) we hold the fortnightly recitations of the discipline – the Pātimokkha. Fittingly, a stone was set into the earth with the straightforward inscription "Vinayo Sāsanassa Āyu" (Vinaya discipline is the life of the religion). The other principal use of the *sima* – for ordinations – was made possible by Ven. Anandamaitreya on the same afternoon that he created it, when be conferred *thera sammati* – the authority of an *upajjhāya** – on Ven. Sumedho. On July 16th three anagarikas were ordained as bhikkhus there, bringing the total up to eleven. With this number it became possible to move people around, and the Ajahn responded to requests by authorizing a branch monastery at Harnham in Northumberland on June 23rd.

This monastery, originally an old farm-worker's cottage, has also grown in the last four years, until for the Vassa of 1987 there were five resident bhikkhus and two anagarikas there. Currently, they are hard at work converting the building and adjacent barns and cottages into a large Dhamma centre for the North of England and the Scottish Borders.

This is one project among many for a Sangha that has diffused throughout Britain, as it and its support, has grown. Local Buddhists set up a small monastery in Devon in 1983, which now acts as a centre for that region; and in 1984, the Amaravati Buddhist Centre was established in Hertfordshire as a national centre, on the initiative of the English Sangha Trust.

An important consideration in the creation of Amaravati was the provision of more facilities for lay people. Until this time, the Sangha generally travelled away from the monastery on invitation to teach, and retreats almost always were held in hired premises. This meant that we were using accommodation that was not specifically designed with Dhamma

---

* Upajjhāya, or preceptor – a bhikkhu of more than ten rains who has the authority to confer full ordination into the Buddhist monkhood.

practice in mind, and so lacked the supportive qualities of a monastery; it also meant that retreatants had to cover the (frequently high) costs of facilities that were intended for rather different activities.

For his part, Ajahn Sumedho had a few further ideas in mind — a place that had a meeting hall large enough to hold the many people wishing to come to public talks and special occasions; enough living space for large numbers of guests to stay with the community and participate in their life of practice; and suitable residences for the increasing number of men and women asking for the Going Forth into the Holy Life.

Out of these wishes and a few minor miracles, Amaravati was born. Formally opened under the auspices of Venerable Anandamaitreya and Tan Chao Khun Paññananda in May 1985, Amaravati — 'The Deathless Realm' — occupies the grounds and the spacious wooden buildings of the former St. Margaret's School in Great Gaddesden. The Centre has a resident monastic community of about forty men and women under the guidance of Ajahn Sumedho, and any number of guests on site living as part of the community, taking part in organized retreats in the separate retreat facility, or here for a public talk, festival or children's class. Once a year — in the same way that Chithurst has the bhikkhu ordinations — Amaravati is the setting for women to ask for the Going Forth as Ten Precept nuns (Siladharas). So, with a mendicant lifestyle now available for women, the Holy Life is developing in conventional form as well as in numbers.

And even as we are coming to terms with the possibilities that Amaravati has created, another branch monastery has opened and is flourishing in Stokes Valley, near Wellington, New Zealand; a branch monastery is being established near Bern, Switzerland; and there are invitations to set up forest monasteries in America.

Relating to all this is awesome at times, because the life of the Sangha is nourished by something far larger than the energies of individual monks and nuns. We realise that Buddhism is providing for a spiritual need in a large number of Western people although its conventions are undemonstrative and our Sangha is quite young. With the sense of responsibility that this creates in the minds of the bhikkhus and siladharas there is lot of effort going into supporting the faith of lay people, and into keeping the monastic training firm enough to make us fit for such responsibility. People living the household life have developed their practice in like fashion, and make full use of the monasteries. In fact, of the few ceremonial occasions that we have during the year, the largest is the *Kathina,* which can only be organised by lay people. Moreover, the *Kathina* is simply an occasion for offering requisites to the bhikkhus — and yet this ceremony draws an attendance that far exceeds our normal number of visitors. People seem to get a lot of joy out of giving to those who are 'worthy of gifts.' To find happiness in giving rather than gaining something is quite a turn-around in many people's attitude towards life, a change of heart that is one of the blessings of a mature and sensitive relationship between Sangha and laity.

What we have all realised, to our surprise, is the extent to which people are willing to live and support the Holy Life. The difficulty hitherto has been in finding places where people could live as monks and nuns, and it wasn't until *that* was given highest priority that the Sangha was able to survive. Rather than try to find ways to adapt the Sangha to Western conditions, Ajahn Sumedho considered it more important to establish the monastic life according to Vinaya and tradition, and allow it to adapt gradually — the way that it has done over the centuries in Asian countries. As always, a high standard of conduct is maintained; and with the native familiarity of most members of the Sangha with the ways of society in the West, people are finding the guidance and example of the community very relevant for their present circumstances.

Meanwhile at Chithurst, the forest is gradually being restored through the planting of thousands of native hardwood trees. It offers an ideal environment for meditation huts, and bhikkhus now may spend the entire Vassa living in the forest and receiving their daily alms-food from local villagers. Several *tudong* walks (long distance pilgrimages) have taken place, including one by the nuns in 1984 to move from Chithurst to Amaravati; this practice seems set to establish itself in the West, as it has done in Thailand.

However, living in the Dhamma makes one's outlook practical and immediate; the future is the unknown, and for now we can only practise what we do know and aspire to live with a quiet heart.

'Where there is uprightness, wisdom is there, and where there is wisdom, uprightness is there. To the upright there is wisdom, to the wise there is uprightness, and wisdom and goodness are declared to be the best things in the world.'

Dīgha Nikāya IV—124

RELIGIOUS CONVENTION AND SILA PRACTICE

I would like to say a few words about the uses of conventional religion. Of course, I am only speaking from my own experience as a Buddhist monk, although I would say that in this respect one can recognize the value of religious convention in whatever form. Nowadays there is a tendency to think that religious convention and form are no longer necessary. There is a kind of hope that if you can just be mindful and know yourself then that is all you need to do. Anyhow, that's how we would like it, isn't it? Just be mindful, throughout the day, throughout the night, whatever you are doing : drinking your whisky, smoking your marijuana cigarette, picking a safe open, mugging someone you met in Soho – as long as it's done mindfully it's all right.

There is a brilliant Buddhist philosopher in Thailand who is quite old now, but I went to stay at his monastery a few years ago. I was coming from Ajahn Chah's monastery, so I asked him about the rules of the monastic order *(Vinaya)* and how important these were in the practice of meditation and enlightenment.

"Well," he said, "only mindfulness—that's all you need. Just be mindful and everything is all right, you know. Don't worry about those other things."

And I thought : "That sounds great, but I wonder why Ajahn Chah emphasises all these rules?"

I had great respect for Ajahn Chah so when I went back I told him what the philosopher-bhikkhu had told me. Ajahn Chah said "That's true,but it's not right."*

---

* i.e. although the statement is quite correct, taken out of context it could be used – as the desana points out – to justify any actions. Similarly the meticulous 'mindfulness practice' described later can also be used unskillfully. Ajahn Sumedho is not criticising these views but pointing to the danger of attaching to *any* view.

Now we are prone to having blind attachments, aren't we? For example, you're locked up in a foul, stinking prison cell and the Buddha comes and says; "Here's the key. All you have to do is take it and put it in the hole there underneath the door handle, turn it to the right, turn the handle, open the door, walk out and you're free."

But you might be so used to being locked up in prison that you didn't quite understand the directions and you say: "Oh, the Lord has given me this key"— and you hang it on the wall and pray to it every day. It might make your stay in prison a little more happy ; you might be able to endure all the hardships and the stench of your foul-smelling cell a little better; but you're still in the cell because you haven't understood that it wasn't the key in itself that was going to save you. Due to lack of intelligence and understanding you just grasped the key blindly. That's what happens in all religion : we just grasp the key, worship it, pray to it.....*but we don't actually learn to use it.*

So then the next time the Buddha comes and says, "Here's the key", you're disillusioned and say; "I don't believe any of this. I've been praying for years to that key and not a thing! *That Buddha is a liar!"* And you take the key and throw it out of the window. That's the other extreme, isn't it? But you're still in the prison cell so that hasn't solved the problem either, has it?

Anyway, a few years later the Buddha comes again and says, "Here's the key", and this time you're a little more wise and you recognise the possibility of using it effectively, so you listen a little more closely, do the right thing and get out.

So the key is like religious convention, like Theravāda Buddhism: it's only a key, only a form; it's not an end in itself. We have to consider, to contemplate how to use it. *What is it for?* We also have to expend the energy to get up, walk over to the door, insert the key into the lock, turn it in the right direction, turn the knob, open the door and walk out. The key isn't going to do that for us; it's something we have to comprehend for ourselves. The convention itself can't do it because it's not capable of making the effort; it doesn't have the vigour or anything of its own other than that which you put into it—just like the key can't do anything by itself. Its usefulness depends on your efforts and wisdom.

Some modern day religious leaders tend to say: "Don't have anything to do with any religious convention. They're all like the walls of prison cells"—and they seem to think that maybe the way is to just get rid of the key. Now, if you're already outside the cell of course you don't need the key. But if you're still inside then it does help a bit!

So I think you have to know whether you're in or out; then you'll know what to do. If you still find you're full of doubt, uncertainty, fear, confusion, (mainly doubt is the real sign); if you're unsure of where you are, what to do or how to do anything; if you're unsure of how to get out of the prison cell then the wisest thing to do is, rather than throwing away keys or just collecting them, take one key and figure out how to use it. That's what we mean by meditation practice. The practice of the *Dhamma* is learning to take a particular key and use it to open the door and walk out. Once you're out then there's no more. Then you know. There's no more doubt.

Now, we can start from the high kind of attitude that mindfulness is enough but then what do we mean by that? *What is mindfulness really?* Is it actually what we believe it to be? We see people who say, "I'm being very mindful", and they're doing something in a very methodical, meticulous way. They're taking in each bite of food and they're lifting, lifting; chewing, chewing, chewing, swallowing, swallowing, swallowing.........

So you think, "He eats very mindfully, doesn't he?", but he *may* not be mindful at all actually. He's just doing it in a very concentrated way: he's concentrating on lifting, on touching, on chewing and on swallowing. We confuse mindfulness with concentration.

Like robbing a bank: we think, "Well, if you rob a bank mindfully, it's all right. I'm very mindful when I rob banks, so there's no *Kamma*". You have to have good powers of concentration to be a good bank robber. You have to have mindfulness in the sense of fear conditions, of being aware of dangers and possibilities—a mind that's on the alert for any kind of movement or sign of danger or threat....and then concentrating your mind on breaking the safe open and so forth. But in the Buddhist sense, mindfulness is always combined with *Paññā*, "mindfulness-wisdom"; *Sati-sampajañña* and *Satipaññā* —they use those two words together in Thailand. They mean "mindfulness and clear comprehension" and "mindfulness - wisdom". Which means that I might have an impulse to rob a bank—"I need some money so I'll go rob the National Westminster Bank"—but the *Satipañña* says, "No, don't act on that impulse!" *Pañña* recognises the bad result if I acted on such an impulse, the *Kammic* result; it confers the understanding that such a thing is wrong, not right to do.

So there's full comprehension of that impulse, knowing it as just an impulse and not self; so that even though I might have the desire to rob a bank I'm not going to make neurotic problems for myself out of worrying about those criminal tendencies. One recognizes that there's just an impulse in the mind that one refrains from acting upon. Then one has a standard of *Sila*** always as a conventional foundation for living in the human form in this society, with other beings, within this material world—a standard or guideline for both action and non-action.

The Five Precepts consist of not killing; not stealing; refraining from wrong kinds of sexual activities; not lying or indulging in false speech; and not taking drink or drugs that change consciousness. These are the guidelines.

Now, *Sila* in Buddhism isn't a rigid, inflexible kind of standard in which you're condemned to hell if you in any way modify anything whatsoever—as you have in that rigid, hard morality we all associate with Victorian times. We all fear that kind of prudish, puritanical morality that used to exist, so that sometimes you say the word "morality" now and everybody shudders and thinks, *"Ugh—Victorian prude!* He's probably some terrible moralistic person who's afraid of life. We have to go out and experience life. *We don't want morality—we want experience!"*

So you see people going out and doing all kinds of things, thinking that experience in itself is all that's necessary. But there are some experiences which it's actually better not to have—especially if they're against the ordinary interpretation of the Five Precepts.

For example, you might say, "I really want to experience

---

* Sila = virtue, as defined by the Five Precepts

murdering someone because my education in life won't be complete until I have. My full freedom to act spontaneously will be inhibited until I actually experience murder."

Some people might believe that....well, perhaps not so much for murder because that's a really heavy one—but they do for other things. They do everything they desire to do and have no standard for saying *No*.

"Don't ever say *No* to anything," they say. "Just say *Yes,* go out and do it and be mindful of it, learn from it......*Experience everything!*"

If you do that you'll find yourself rather jaded, worn out, confused, miserable and wretched even at a very young age. When you see some of the pathetic cases I've seen—young people, you know, who went out and experienced everything, and you say:

"How old are you? *Forty?*"

And they say, "No, actually I'm *twenty one.*"

It sounds good, doesn't it? *Do everything you desire*—that's what we'd like to hear. I would. It would be nice to do everything I desire, never have to say *No*. But then in a few years you also begin to reflect that desires have no end. What you desire now, you want something more than that next time and there's no end to it. You might be temporarily gratified, like when you eat too much food and can't stand to eat another bite; then you look at the most delicious gourmet preparations and you say:

"Oh, disgusting!"

But it's only momentary revulsion and it doesn't take long before they start looking all right again.

In Thailand, Buddhism is an extremely tolerant kind of religion; moralistic attitudes have never really developed there. This is why people are sometimes upset when they go to Bangkok and hear horrendous stories of child prostitution and corruption and so on. Bangkok is the Sin City of the World these days. You say "Bangkok" and everybody's eyes either light up or else they look terribly upset and say:

"How can a Buddhist country allow such terrible things to go on?"

But then knowing Thailand one recognizes that, although they may be a bit lax and loose on some levels, at least there isn't the kind of militant cruelty there that you find in some other countries where they line all the prostitutes up and shoot them and kill all the criminals in the name of their religion. *In Thailand one begins to appreciate that morality really has to come from* wisdom, *not from fear.*

So some Thai monks will teach morality on a less strict basis than others: In the matter of the first guideline or *sīla,* non-killing: *(Pānātipātā)* I know a monk who lives on the sea coast of the Gulf of Thailand in an area where there are a lot of pirates and fishermen, who are a very rough, crude kind of people. Murder is quite common among them. So this monk just tries to encourage them not to kill each other. When these people come to the monastery he doesn't go round raising non-killing to the level of "You shouldn't kill anything - not even a mosquito larva" because they couldn't accept that. Their livelihood depends very much on fishing and the killing of animals.

What I'm presenting isn't morality on a rigid standard or that's too difficult to keep, but rather as a way for you to reflect upon and use so that you begin to understand it and how to live in a better way. If you start out taking too strict a position you either become very moralistic, puritanical and attached, or else you think you can't do it, so you don't bother;you have no standard at all.

Now the second precept is refraining from stealing. On the coarsest level, say, you refrain from just robbing banks, shop-lifting and things like that. But then if you refine your *Sīla* more you refrain from taking things which have not been given to you. As monks we refrain even from touching things that are not given to us. If we go into your home we're not supposed to go around picking up and looking at things, even though we have no intention of taking them away with us. Even food has to be offered directly to us: if you set it down and say, "This is for you," if we stick to our rules we're not supposed to eat it until you offer it directly to us. That's a refinement of the precept to not take anything that's not been given *(Adinnādānā).*

So there's the coarse aspect of just refraining from the most gross kinds of theft or burglary; and a more refined training—a way of training yourself.

Now I found this a very helpful monastic rule because I was very heedless as a layman. Somebody would invite me to their home and I'd be looking at this, looking at that, touching this; going into shops, picking up this and that—I didn't even know that it was wrong or might annoy anybody. It was a habit. And then when I was ordained as a monk I couldn't do that any more and I'd sit there and feel this impulse to look at this and pick that up, but I'd have these precepts saying I couldn't do that.....And like food: somebody would put down food and I'd just grab it and start eating. But through the monastic training you develop a much more graceful way of behaving. Then you sit down and after a while you don't feel the urge to pick up things or grab hold of them. You can wait. And then people can offer, which is a much more beautiful way of relating to things around you and to other people than habitually grabbing, touching, eating and so on.

Then there's the third precept about sexuality *(Kāmesu Micchācārā)*. The idea at the present time is that any old kind of sexuality is experience so it's all right to do—just so long as you're mindful! And somehow not having sexual relations is seen as some kind of terrible perversity.

On the coarsest level this precept means refraining from adultery: from being unfaithful to your spouse. But then you can refine that within marriage to where you're becoming more considerate, less exploitive, less obsessed with sexuality so you're no longer using it merely for bodily pleasure. You can in fact refine it right down to celibacy: to where you're living like a Buddhist monk and no kind of sexual activity is allowed. This is the range, you see, within the precepts.

A lot of people think that the celibate monastic life must be a terrible repression. But it's not, because sexual urges are fully accepted and understood as being natural urges, only they're not acted upon. You can't help having sexual desires. You can't say, "I won't have any more of that kind of desire....." Well, you can say it but you still do! If you're a monk and you think you shouldn't have anything like that then you become a very frightened and repressed kind of monk.

I've heard some monks say: "I'm just not worthy of the robe. People shouldn't give me alms food. I'll have to disrobe because I've got so many bad thoughts going through my mind."

The robe doesn't care about your thoughts! Don't make a problem out of it. We all have nasty thoughts going through our minds when we're in these robes, just like everybody else. But we train ourselves not to speak or act upon them. When we've taken the *Pātimokkha* discipline, we accept those things, recognize them, are fully conscious of them, let them go—and they cease. Then after a while one finds a great peacefulness in one's mind as a result of the celibate life.

Sexual life on the other hand is very exciting. If you're really upset, frightened, bored, restless, then your mind very easily goes into sexual fantasies. Violence is very exciting too, so often sex and violence are put together, as in rape and things of that nature. People like to look at those things at the cinema. If they made a film about a celibate monk keeping the *Vinaya* discipline, very few people would appreciate that! It would be a very boring film. But if they made a film about a monk who breaks all the precepts, they'd make a fortune!

The fourth precept is on speech, *Musāvādā;* on the coarsest level, if you're a big liar, say, just keep this precept by refraining from telling big lies. If you take that precept then at least every time you tell a big lie you'd know it, wouldn't you? But if you don't take any precept sometimes you can tell big lies and not even know you're doing it. It becomes a habit. Then if you refine this from the coarse position to a refined one, you learn to speak and use communication in a very careful and responsible way. You're not just chattering, babbling, gossiping, exaggerating; you're not being terribly clever or using speech to hurt or insult or disparage other people in any intentional way. You begin then to recognize how very deeply we do affect one another with the things we say. We can ruin whole days for each other by saying unkind things.

The fifth precept is *Surāmeraya majjapamādatthānā:* refraining from alcoholic drinks and drugs which change consciousness. Now, that can be on the level of just refraining from drunkenness—that's what everybody likes to think it means! But then the sober side of you says you maybe shouldn't have a drink of any kind; not even a glass of wine with your dinner. It's a standard to reflect upon and use.

If you've committed yourself to these precepts, then you know when you've broken them. So they're guidelines to being a little more alert, a little more awake and also more responsible about how you live. If we don't have standards then we just tend to do what we feel like doing, or what someone else feels like doing.

I have a very natural kind of moral nature. I've never really liked being immoral. But when I lived in Berkeley, California, because the more clever, intelligent and experienced beings around me that I greatly admired seemed to fully commend immoralities, I thought: "Well, maybe I should do that too....." Certainly when you're looking up to somebody, you want to be like them. I got myself into a terrible mess because people can be very convincing. They can make murder sound like a sacred act!

So *Sīla* is a guide, a way of anchoring yourself in refraining from unskillful actions with your body and speech, both in regard to yourself and to the other beings around you. *It's not a kind of absolute standard.* I'm not telling you that if you kill a worm in your garden you'll be reborn in the next 10,000 lifetimes as a worm in order to frighten you into not killing. There's no wisdom in that. If you're just conditioned then you're just doing it because you're afraid you'll go to hell. You don't really *understand;* you've not reflected and watched and really used your wisdom to observe how things are.

If you're frightened of action and speech then you'll just become neurotic; but on the other hand if you're not frightened enough and think you can do anything, then you'll also become confused and neurotic!

Sigmund Freud had all kinds of people coming to him with terrible hang-ups and as sexual repression was the ordinary thing in Europe and America at the time, he thought: "Well, if we just stop repressing, then we won't have these problems any more. We'll become free, happy, well-integrated personalities."

But nowadays there's no restriction any more—and you still get hysterical, miserable, neurotic people! So it's obvious that these are two extremes springing from a lack of mindfulness in regard to the natural condition of sexuality.

We have to recognize both what's exciting and what's calming. Buddhist meditation—why is this so boring? Repetitions and chanting......why don't we sing arias? I could do it! I've always wanted to be an opera singer. But on the conventional level of propriety or when I'm sitting on the high seat doing my duty, then I chant in monotone as best I can. If you really concentrate on monotone chanting, it's tranquilizing.

One night we were sitting in our forest monastery in Thailand, meditating, when I heard an American pop song that I really hated when I was a layman. It was being blasted out by one of those medicine sellers who go to all the villages in big vans with loudspeakers that play this kind of music in order to attract the villagers to come and buy their quacky medicines. The wind was blowing in the right direction and the sound of *Tell Laura I Love Her* seemed right there in the meditation hall itself. I hadn't heard American pop music for so many years so while this smarmy, sentimental song was playing I was actually beginning to cry! And I began to recognize the tremendous emotional pull of that kind of music. If you don't really understand it, it grabs your heart and you get caught up in the excitement and emotion of it. This is the effect of music when we're not mindful.

So chanting is monotone because if you concentrate on it it's not going to carry you away into sentimental feelings: into tears or ecstasy. Instead you feel tranquil, peaceful, serene. *Ānāpānasati** tranquilizes too because it has a gentle rhythm—subtle, not exciting. And the monastic life itself is boring in the sense of lacking romance, adventure and excitement. But it is tranquilizing, peaceful, calming......

Therefore reflect in your life upon what excites and what calms, so that you begin to understand how to use *Paññā:* your wisdom faculty. As Buddhists we do this so that we know what's affecting us. We understand the forces of nature with which we have to coexist. We can't control everything so that nothing violent or exciting ever happens around us. But we can understand it. We can put forward some effort towards understanding and learning from our lives as we live them.

---

* A widely used meditation technique whereby one composes the mind by focussing attention on the inhalation and exhalation of breath.

'Truly wisdom springs from meditation;
without meditation, wisdom wanes;
having known these two paths
of progress and decline,
let one conduct oneself
so that wisdom may increase.'

Dhammapada 282

SKILLFUL MEANS

1. -- Letting Go

We have been discussing the First Noble Truth – suffering – which becomes increasingly apparent as you sit here contemplating your own body and mind. Just be aware of what happens: you can see that when good thoughts pass by, or physical pleasure, there's happiness, and when there's pain or negativity, there's despair. So we can see we're always habitually trying to attain, or maintain, or get rid of, conditions. The Second Noble Truth is that of being aware of the arising of the three different kinds or desire that we have – desire for sense pleasure, for becoming, or for getting rid of something - and how this arises according to conditions. The penetration of the Third Noble Turth is to see how that which arises has a cessation. We become aware of the cessation, the letting go, and thus we develop the Fourth Noble Truth, the Truth of the Eightfold Path – right understanding, right intention, right speech, right action, right livelihood, right effort, right mindfulness and right concentration – in other words the path of awareness.

To be aware we have to use skillful means, because at first we're mystified by this. We tend to conceive awareness and try to *become* aware, thinking that awareness is something we have to *get* or *attain* or try to develop; but this very intention, this very conceptualisation.... makes us heedless! We keep trying to become mindful rather than just being aware of our mind as it tries to become and tries to attain, following the three kinds of desire that cause us suffering.

The practice of 'letting go' is very effective for minds obsessed by compulsive thinking: you simplify your meditation practice down to just two words- 'letting go'- rather than try to develop *this* practice and then develop *that;* and achieve *this* and go into *that,* and understand *this,* and read the Suttas, and study the Abhidhamma.....and then learn Pāli and Sanskrit.... then the Madhyamika and the Prajna Paramita.....get ordinations in the Hinayana, Mahayana, Vajrayana.... write books and become a world renowned authority on Buddhism. Instead of becoming the world's expert on Buddhism and being invited to great International Buddhist Conferences, just 'let go, let go, let go'. I did nothing but this for about two years – every time I tried to understand or figure things out, I'd say 'let go, let go', until the desire would fade out. So I'm making it very simple for you to save you from getting caught in incredible amounts of suffering. There's nothing more sorrowful than having to attend International Buddhist Conferences! Some of you might have the desire to become the Buddha of the age, Maitreya, radiating love throughout the world -- but instead I suggest just being an earthworm, letting go of the desire to radiate love throughout the world. Just be an earthworm who knows only two words- 'let go, let go, let go'. You see, ours is the Lesser Vehicle,the Hinayana, so we only have these simple, poverty-stricken practices!

The important thing in meditation practice is to be constant and resolute in the practice, determined to be enlightened. This is not to be conceited or foolish, but resolute, even when the going is rough. Remind yourself of Buddha, Dhamma, Sangha and stay with it, letting go of despair, letting go of anguish, letting go of pain, of doubt, of everything that arises and passes that we habitually cling to and identify with. Keep this 'letting go' like a constant refrain in your mind so it just pops up on its own, no matter where you are.

At first we have to obsess our minds with this, because our minds are obsessed with all kinds of useless things - with worries about this and that, with doubt, with anger, vindictiveness, jealousy, fear, dullness and stupidity of various kinds. We have obsessive minds that are obsessed with things that cause us pain and lead us into difficulties in life. Our society has taught us how to fill up the mind, jam it full of ideas, prejudices, regrets, anticipations and expectations - it is a society for filling up vessels. When you look at the book stores here in Oxford, filled up with all the information you could possibly want to know, published in very nice bindings with pictures and illustrations... or we can fill our minds by watching T.V., go to the cinema, read the newspapers... That's a good way to fill your mind up - but look at what's printed in the newspapers! It appeals to people's lower instincts and drives - all about violence, wars, corruption and perversities... and gossip. All this has its effect and suggestion on the mind. As long as our minds are obsessed with facts, symbols and conventions, then if we stuff any more into it, it becomes jam-packed full and we have to go crazy. We can go out and get drunk - it's a way of letting go! What do you think pubs are for? There we can dare to say all the things we want to say but don't have the nerve to say when sober. We can be irrational, be silly, laugh and cavort *"Because I was drunk, I was under the influence of alcohol."*

When we don't understand the nature of things, we are very suggestible. You see in our society how suggestion works on teenagers. Now it's the punk rock generation - everybody in that generation thinks of themselves as punks and acts like it. Fashions are all suggestion - for women, you are not beautiful unless you are dressed in a certain way. Cinema films suggest all kinds of delights to the senses, and we think maybe we should try that, maybe we are missing something if we aren't experiencing it... It's so bad now that nobody knows what is beautiful or ugly anymore. Somebody says that harmony is cacophony, and if you don't know and are still subject to suggestion, you believe that. Even if you don't believe at first, it begins to work on your mind so you start thinking *"Maybe it is that way, maybe immorality is morality, and morality is immorality"*.

We feel obliged to know all kinds of things - to understand and to try to convince others. You hear my talks, you read books, and you want to tell others about Buddhism - you might even feel a bit evangelical after the retreat – but keep letting go of even the desire to tell others. When we feel enthusiastic, we begin to impose on other people; but in meditation we let go of the desire to influence others until the right time for it occurs– then it happens naturally rather than as an aggressive ambition.........So you do the things that need to be done, and you let go: when people tell you you should read *this* book and *that* book, take *this* course and *that* course...study Pali, the Abhidhamma...go into the history of Buddhism, Buddhist logic...and on and on like that...'let go, let go, let go'. If you fill your mind with more concepts and opinions, you are just increasing your ability to doubt. It's only through learning how to empty the mind out that you can fill it with things of value – and learning how to empty a mind takes a great deal of wisdom.

Here in this meditation retreat, the suggestions I am giving you are for skillful means. The obsession of 'letting go' is a skillful one – as you repeat this over and over, whenever a thought arises, you are *aware* of its arising. You keep letting go of whatever moves, and if it doesn't go, don't try to force it. This 'letting go' practice is a way of clearing the mind of its obsessions and negativity – use it gently but with resolution. Meditation is a *skillful* letting go, deliberately emptying out the mind so we can see the purity of the mind; cleaning it out so we can put the right things in it. You respect your mind, so you are more careful what you put in it – like if you have a nice house, you don't go out and pick up all the filth from the street and bring it in, you bring in things that will enhance it and make it a refreshing and delightful place.

If you are going to identify with anything, then don't identify with mortal conditions. See what identification is - investigate your own mind to see clearly the nature of thought, of memory, of sense consciousness, and of feeling as impermanent conditions. Bring your awareness to the slower things, to the transiency of bodily sensation; investigate pain and see it as a moving energy, a changing condition. Emotionally it seems permanent when you are in pain, but that is just an illusion of the emotions – let go of it all. Even if you have insight, even if you understand everything clearly - let go of the insight.

When the mind is empty, say *'Who is it that lets go?'* Ask the question, try to find out who it is, what it is that lets go. Bring up that not-knowing state with the word 'Who?' - *'Who am I? Who lets go?'* A state of uncertainty arises, bring this up, allow it to be.....and there is emptiness, voidness, the state of uncertainty when the mind just goes blank.

So I keep stressing this right understanding, right attitude, right intention; more towards simplifying your life so that you aren't involved in unskillful and complex activitives, so that you don't live heedlessly, exploiting others and having no respect for yourself or the people around you. Develop the Precepts as a standard, and *nekkhamma* - renunciation of that which is unskillful or unnecessary - and then mentally let go of greed, let go of hatred, let go of delusion. This is not being averse to these conditions; it is letting go of them when you find you are attached. When you are suffering- *'Why am I suffering? Why am I miserable?' Because you are clinging to something!* Find out what you are clinging to to get to the source. *'I'm unhappy because nobody loves me.'* That may be true, maybe nobody loves you, but the unhappiness comes from wanting people to love you. Even if they do love you, you will still have suffering if you think that other people are responsible for your happiness or your suffering. Someone says *'You are the greatest person in the world!'* - and you jump for joy. Someone says - *'You are the most horrible person I've met in my life!'* - and you get depressed. Let go of depression, let go of happiness. Keep the practice simple - live your life mindfully, morally, and have faith in letting go.

It's important for you to realise that none of us are helpless victims of fate. We are as long as we remain ignorant. As long as you remain ignorant, you are a helpless victim of your ignorance. All that is ignorant is born and dies, it is bound to die - that's all, it's caught in the cycle of death and rebirth. And if *you* die, *you* will be reborn - you can count on it, and the more heedlessly you live your life, the worse the rebirth. So the Buddha taught a way to break the cycle, and that's through awareness, through seeing the cycle rather than being attached to it. When you let go of the cycle, then you are no longer harmed by it. So you let go of the cycle, let go of birth and death, let go of becoming: letting go of desire is the development of the Third Noble Truth which leads to the Eightfold Path.

2 -- Listening to the mind

In this form of meditation practice, listen inwardly and listen carefully. To listen inwardly, regard the outside of things as totally unimportant — go beyond the concepts and thoughts; they are not you. Listen to that which is around the words themselves, the silence, the space. Now, when you listen, what do you hear? Listen to these changing things like it's somebody else talking, saying, "I don't like this or that; I'm bored, fed-up; I want to go home." Or listen to the religious fanatic or the cynic; whatever the form or the quality of the voice, we can still be aware of its changing nature. You can't have a permanent desire. In listening inwardly until we are listening all the time, we begin to experience emptiness. Normally, we don't listen, and we think we *are* these voices, creating terrible problems for ourselves by identifying with the voices of desire. We *think* there is a permanent personality or being, with permanent greed; but in meditation, we can *see* that these voices arise out of the void - they arise, and they pass away.

Following the teaching of the Buddha, the practice is to know the known. To know *what*? What do Buddhas know; what does the One Who Knows know anyway? The One Who Knows knows that these changing conditions are not self. There is not any eternal or soul-like quality, no substance in these things that one could call a permanent possession. The One Who Knows knows that if it arises, it passes away — you don't have to know any more to be a Buddha. Being the Buddha means knowing, by observing, not by believing the Scriptures, or me. See for yourself. Just try to find a condition that arises that doesn't pass away. Is there something that's born that doesn't die? Be that Buddha who knows, by putting energy into experiencing your life here and now, not by getting lost in the delusion of the *idea* of being Buddha – "I'm the Buddha; I know it all." Sometimes desire even takes the form of a Buddha. Actually there is no-one who knows and to conceive of being Buddha is not just *being* Buddha.

The Theravādins talk about *anattā,* and the Mahayanists talk about *sunyata* — they really mean the same thing. To experience *anattā,* one investigates and sees that the clinging to the ego, to the neuroses that we all have, the thoughts, greed, hatred and delusion, are all *anattā* There is no self to be saved, just empty conditions that arise out of the void and pass back into it with no remainder. So we let things go, allow things to be as they are and they change quite naturally on their own. You don't have to force them. If you're experiencing something unpleasant, you don't have to annihilate it; it will go quite on its own. Self conceit says, "I don't like this condition, I've got to get rid of it, wipe it out." This creates a more complex situation than before — you're trying to push something away, bury your head in the ground and say, "Oh, its gone!". But that desire to get rid of, *vibhavatanhā,* just creates the conditions for it to arise again, because we haven't seen that it dies quite naturally.

Now we're sitting in a room full of kammic formations that we conceive to be permanent personalities. We carry these around like a 'conceptions bag' because on the conventional level of thoughts we regard each other as permanent personalities. How many things do you carry around with you? — grudges against people, infatuations, fears and things of the past? We can get upset just by thinking of the name of someone who has caused us suffering — *"How dare they do that,treat me like that!"* — over something that happened twenty years ago! Some people spend most of their lives carrying grudges around, so that they ruin the *rest* of their lives. But as meditators, we break through the pattern of memory. Instead of remembering people and making them real, we see that in the moment, memory and bitterness are changing conditions; we see that they are *anicca, dukkha, anattā.* They are formed in time, just like the sand grains of the Ganges River — whether they are beautiful, ugly, black or white, sand grains is all that they are. So listen inwardly. Listen to the mind when you're starting to experience pain in the body; bring up the voice that says, "I don't want this pain, when is the darned bell going to ring?" Listen to the moaning, discontented voice — or listen when you get really high, "Oh bliss, I feel so wonderful". Listen to the *devata* indulging in bliss and happiness, take the position of the silent listener, making no preferences between *devatas* and devilish things; and remember that if it's a condition, it ends.

Recognise and let things come and go — these are just kammic conditions changing, so don't interfere. The tendency of the modern mind is to think that there's some ogre lurking way down deep inside, just waiting for an unguarded moment to overwhelm you and drive you permanently insane. Some people actually live their whole lives with that kind of fear, and every time the monster starts to come up: *"Oh — oh........!"* But monsters are just another *sankhara,* another grain of sand of the Ganges River. Maybe an ugly sand grain, but that's all. If you're going to get upset every time you see an ugly sand grain, you're going to find life increasingly more difficult. Sometimes we have to accept the fact that some sand grains are ugly. Let them *be* ugly; don't get upset. If you saw me sitting beside the Ganges River looking at ugly sand grains, saying, "I'm going to go *crazy!*" you'd think, "Ajahn Sumedho *is* crazy!" Even a *really* ugly sand grain is just a sand grain.

So what we're doing is looking at the common factor of all these different qualities — hidden monsters, latent repressed energies and powers and archetypal forces — they are all just *sankhāras;* nothing much. You take the position of the Buddha: being the knowing. Even the unknown we see as just another changing condition — sometimes there's knowing, sometimes not knowing; one conditions the other. The black hole, sunlight, night and day are all change; there's no self, nothing to become if you're being the knowing. But if you're reacting to all the qualities of *samsāra* you get really neurotic, that's endless, just like reacting to all the sand grains of the Ganges River. How many life times does it take to react to all the sand grains of the Ganges River? Do you think you have to emotionally respond to each sand grain of the Ganges River, being ecstatic over the beautiful and depressed over the ugly ones? Yet that's what people do, they dull themselves, get worn down and exhausted with this emotional turmoil all the time and want to annihilate themselves. So they start taking drugs, drinking all the time to desensitise themselves. What we are doing, instead of building a shell and hiding ourselves away in fear and dullness, is to observe that none of this is self. So we don't have to desensitise ourselves, we can become even more sensitive, clear and bright. In that clarity and brightness there is the knowing that if it arises, it passes away — and that's what Buddhas know!

Ajahn Sumedho as dhutanga bhikkhu

'Just as, O king, the bhikkhu, so long as these Five Hindrances are not put away within him, looks upon himself as in debt, diseased, in prison, in slavery, lost on a desert road. But when these Five Hindrances have been put away within him, he looks upon himself as freed from debt, rid of disease, out of jail, a free man and secure .. .'

Digha Nikāya II — 73

THE FIVE HINDRANCES

In meditation one develops an understanding of the Five Hindrances* - how when one of them is present, you investigate it, you understand it, you accept its presence and you learn how to deal with it. Sometimes you can just tell it to go away and it goes; sometimes you just have to allow it to be there till it wears out. We have subtle ways of being averse to that which is unpleasant and we tend not to be very honest about our intentions. Our habits are that as soon as something unpleasant arises we try to move away from it or destroy it. So long as we are doing this, we don't have any *"Samādhi"* or concentration. It is only when these Five Hindrances are absent, or we are no longer attached to them, that we find any peace of mind or a concentrated heart. It is only in the moment when a hindrance actually arises that we can really penetrate it and have insight. If you have noticed, you may go to some of these lectures and gain a profound understanding of the *Dhamma,* but you can still get angry or frightened or feel desire for things; when the actual situation arises you are not mindful, you tend to resist or resent or just indulge.

I spent my first year as a *Samanera* living in a monastery in

---

* The Five Hindrances - obstacles on the spiritual path - are :
1. Sense desire/'greed' (Kāmacchanda)
2. Ill - will (vyāpāda)
3. Dullness/sloth (thīna - middha)
4. Restlessness/worry (uddhacca - kukkucca)
5. Doubt (vicikicchā)
   In characteristic style, Ven. Sumedho talks about these, rather than delivering a systematic lecture. Owing to the time-limit of the talk, restlessness/worry was not commented on.

North East Thailand. I was not compelled to do anything other than just live in a little hut. The monks brought me food every day and, as I could speak no Thai and nobody spoke any English, I didn't have to talk to anyone. The senses were therefore not stimulated to any great extent, so sensory deprivation set in and I found myself becoming very tranquil — so tranquil, in fact, that I attained great states of bliss and ecstasy. I'd sit on the porch of my little *kuti* (hut) and tears of love would well up in my eyes for the mosquitoes which were biting me. I could think in abstract terms about "all beings everywhere" and feel great love for them too. I even forgave my enemies and those who had caused me suffering in the past. I could entertain these high-minded feelings for "all beings" mainly because I was not having to live with them.

Then one day I had to go to the Immigration to renew my visa. I had to travel to a place called Nong Khai, which is where you cross the Mekong River to go to Laos. Because of my new sensitive state, as I walked to the town I could see things more clearly than ever before. I saw the sorrow and anguish in the faces of the people. And then, when I walked into the Immigration, I felt this iron curtain of hatred forming in front of me. I found out later that the leading monk of the province had ordered the officials to give me a visa. This was not quite in line with the regulations and so had forced the officials into a position that was really quite unfair. Because of this they had a definite aversion towards me and would not grant me a visa, which was very confusing for me because of my heightened state of awareness. The feeling of great love I had for all beings began to fade away very quickly.

By the time I got back to the monastery I was in a frantic mental state. I went to my *kuti* and spent the next three days just calming down all that had been aroused during that hour's visit to the Immigration.

After a few months I became very fond of the isolated life. There's something very romantic about living that way. It's so peaceful not to be exposed to the misery of people or to have your senses excited by their actions. Nature itself is very peaceful, very pleasant to be with. Even the mosquitoes, which you might think must be terribly annoying, are not really anywhere near as annoying as people are. Actually, it takes much less skill to live with mosquitoes than with another person.

I got very attached to that way of life but after a few months I had to go to Bangkok. I remember sitting in the train on the way from Nong Khai to the capital. I didn't want to talk to anyone. I just sat there with my high-minded thoughts about helping all beings, dedicating my life to their welfare, about the *Dhamma* and the Buddha. I was permeated by an overwhelming state of bliss. *"What a wonderful state to be in!"*, I thought. That noisy, confusing and unpleasant city put paid to all that; in half an hour my mind was in terrible confusion.

From these experiences I was beginning to see that the way to enlightenment did not lie in being shut off from everything that was unpleasant, but rather through learning to understand all that we find unpleasant or difficult. Those particular conditions have been set there for a purpose, to teach us. No matter how much we don't want them and would rather like things otherwise, somehow they will persist in our lives until we have understood and transcended them.

My hermit life ended soon after that. I was going to be ordained as a *bhikkhu* and would live with Ajahn Chah at a monastery where I wouldn't be allowed the luxury of ascetic practice. I'd have to live in a community of monks and perform my duties, learn all the disciplinary rules that *bhikkhus* have to learn and live under the authority of someone else. By this time I was quite willing to accept all this; I realised that in fact it was exactly what I needed. I certainly did not need any more ecstatic blissful states that disappeared as soon as anything annoying happened.

At Wat Pah Pong I found a constant stream of annoying conditions coming at me, which gave me a chance of learning to deal with the Five Hindrances. At the other monasteries in Thailand where I'd lived, the fact that I'd been a Westerner had meant that I could expect to have the best of everything. I could also get out of the work and other mundane things that the other monks were expected to do by saying something like: *"I'm busy meditating now. I don't have time to sweep the floor. Let someone else sweep it. I'm a serious meditator."* But when I arrived at Wat Pah Pong and people said, *"He's an American; he can't eat the kind of food we eat,"* Ajahn Chah said, *"He'll have to learn."* And when I didn't like the meditation hut I was given and asked for another that I liked better, Ajahn Chah said, *"No."*

I had to get up at 3 o'clock in the morning and attend Morning Chanting and Meditation. There were readings from the *Vinaya* too. They were read in Thai, which at first I didn't understand; and even when I could understand the language, they were excruciatingly boring to listen to. You'd hear about how a monk who has a rent in his robe so many inches above the hem must have it sewn up before dawn and I kept thinking, *"This isn't what I was ordained for!"* I was caught up in these meticulous rules, trying to figure out whether the hole in my robe was four inches above the hem or not and whether I should have to sew it up before dawn. Or they'd read about making a sitting cloth and the monks would have to know that the border had to be so many inches wide; and there'd be one monk who'd say, *"Well, I've seen a sitting cloth with the border different from that."* And the monks would even become argumentative about the border of that sitting cloth. *"Let's talk about serious things,"* I'd think; *"Things of importance, like the* Dhamma.*"*

When it came to the pettiness of everyday life and of living with people of many different temperaments, problems and characters, whose minds were not necessarily as inspired as mine seemed to be at the time, I felt a great depression. Then I was faced with the Five Hindrances as a practical reality. There was no escape. I had to learn the lesson that they were there to teach.

As for the first hindrance - greed - you would be surprised at some of the forms that takes for monks. As a layman you can spend time trying to seek out suitable objects, you can form material possessions, but because monks live a celibate life and have very few possessions we find our greed accumulates over things like robes or alms bowls. We are allowed one meal a day, so a lot of greed and aversion may arise with regard to food. At Wat Pah Pong we had to accept whatever hut we were given, so sometimes you were fortunate, you got a really nice one, and sometimes you got a not very nice one. But then you could watch the aversion that arose if you were given something you did not like, or the pleasure if you were given something you liked.

I became obsessed with robes for the first few months—the colour of the robe, believe it or not. At the monastery where I lived before, they wore robes of a bright "knock-your-eyes-out" kind of orange – and it was not my colour. When I went to Wat Pah Pong, they wore a kind of ochre yellow or brownish coloured robe, and so I developed great desire for this kind. First they would not give me one; I had to wear one of these "knock-your-eyes-out" orange robes, and I became very greedy to get new robes - big robes. The robes in Thailand never fitted me properly, and at Wat Pah Pong they'd make them to your size, you'd have tailor-made robes. Finally after a month or so Ajahn Chah suggested that a monk make me these robes, but then I became obsessed by the colour. I did not want it too brown and I did not want very much red in it. I went through a lot of sorrow and despair trying to get the right colour for the robe!

Although we could not eat anything in the afternoon, certain things are allowed in the *Vinaya,* and one was sugar. So then I found myself having a fantastic obsession with sweets, while before I had not really cared about sweets at all. At Wat Pah Pong they'd have a sweet drink once every two or three days in the afternoon. And one began to anticipate the day when they would give you tea with sugar in it–or coffee with sugar in it. Or, several times, they'd even make cocoa! When word got around that we'd have cocoa that evening, one could not think about anything else. I did not find sexual desire any problem in those days, because my obsessions were with sugar and sweets. I'd go to bed at night and dream about pastry shops. I'd be sitting at the table just about to put the most gooky pastry in my mouth, and I'd wake up and think: "If only I could get just one bite!"

Before I went to Thailand I had spent a few years in Berkeley, California, where it was pretty much a case of "doing your own thing" There was no sense of having to obey anybody, or live under a discipline of any sort. But at Wat Pah Pong I had to live following a tradition that I did not always like or approve of, in a situation where I had no authority whatsoever. I did not mind obeying Ajahn Chah; I respected him. But sometimes I had to obey monks I did not like very much and who I thought were inferior to me. The Thai monks were very critical of me at Wat Pah Pong, whereas in other monasteries they had praised me all the time. They used to say: "How beautiful you are." It was the first time in my life I'd ever felt that I was a raving beauty. "And what beautiful skin you have". They liked white skin, and though my skin is not really very beautiful, it *is* white. At Wat Pah Pong, however, the monks would say: "You have ugly skin with brown spots." I was in my thirties at the time and still sensitive to the ageing process, and they were asking: "How old are you?" I'd say: "Thirty-three." And they'd say: "Really, we thought you were at least sixty." Then they would criticise the way I walked and say: "You don't walk right. You are not very mindful when you walk." And I'd take this bag - they gave me a bag - and I'd just dump it down, and think, "This can't be very important;" and they'd say: "Put your bag down right. You take it like this, fold it over, and then you set it down beside you like that."

The way I ate, the way I walked, the way I talked - everything was criticised and made fun of, but something made me stay on, and endure through it. I actually learnt how to conform to a tradition and a discipline - and that took a number of years, really, because there was always strong resistance. But I began to understand the wisdom of the discipline of the *Vinaya,* which is not all that apparent on reading the *Vinaya-Pitaka.* Having an opinion on the traditions and the *Vinaya* itself, you think: "This rule isn't necessary." And you could spend hours of your day just rationalizing this, saying: "This is the twentieth century, these things are not necessary." And you would keep watching the discontent and proliferation going on inside you, and you'd ask yourself: "Is this suffering?" Then you'd keep watching the reactions you had to being corrected, criticised, or praised. Over the years equanimity seemed to develop. One found that anger, annoyance and aversion began to fade out. And when your mind no longer inclines towards dwelling in aversion, you begin to have some joy and some peace of mind.

As I gained confidence in the practice and the teacher and then the monastery, I developed a kind of obsessive attachment to it. I couldn't see any faults in it and I felt that this was what everybody should be doing. People would come to the monastery and I'd feel it was my duty to convert them. I can understand how missionaries must feel. You feel very inspired, very attached to something that has helped you and given you happiness and insight. You feel compelled to tell everybody else about it, whether they want to hear it or not. So it was all right as long as the Westerners who came agreed with me. That was nice, I could inspire them and they would feel the same sense of dedication, and we would re-inforce each other. We could get together and talk about our tradition and our teacher being the best, and how we had discovered something wonderful. Then inevitably some negative American or Englishman would come to the monastery and not fall for any of this. This happened very strongly about my fifth year when an American came who had been at the Zen Centre in San Francisco. He proceeded to find fault with Ajahn Chah, with Wat Pah Pong, with Theravada Buddhism, with the *Vinaya* - with everything. He was quite an intelligent person and he had certainly a lot of experience in going from one teacher to another, from one *ashram* to another, from one monastery to another and finding fault with them. So this put doubt into the minds of people: "Maybe there is a better way to do it, a quicker way. Maybe Ajahn Chah is an old-fashioned nobody." There was a teacher in India who was giving meditation courses where people were 'becoming *Sotapannas* almost immediately'. "I don't know if I am a *Sotapanna* yet or not. If I could have a teacher come and tell me, verify, it would be really nice to know where you are in this meditation." Ajahn Chah would not say anything to you. So I felt a strong aversion arise towards this American, I felt the need to tear down every other type of Buddhism, every other teacher, every possible alternative. I became very critical and every time somebody would say: "I know a better system " I would immediately, rather than listen to why it was better, find every possibility of why it was worse. So I developed a habit of tearing down other teachers and traditions. But this brought me no joy. I began to see the suffering in always having to defend something and having to tear down anything that threatens the security you find in attachment.

If you never really understand doubt, the nature of uncertainty in your own mind, then you get overwhelmed by it, and when someone says: "I know a better way, a quicker way", you start doubting: "Maybe there *is* a better way, a quicker way". Then they would describe this better way in very rational terms and you would think: "Well, yes, maybe that's the way to do it." But when you are attached and feel loyal to your teacher, you think: "I can't do that - it's better to do it the slow way and be sure." So then you start putting down anybody who suggests that there is a better way or a quicker way. But the important thing to understand is the doubting mind. I saw that it was not up to me to decide which was the best or the quickest way to do anything, but to understand my own uncertainty. So I began to investigate the mental state that would arise when doubt was put into my mind, and after a while I began to accept any kind of doubt, regarding it as a changing condition.

Once when I was in Bangkok people were comparing religions, and I was trying to be very tolerant and accept that all religions were equally good, even though I did not really think so. I would always try to say something good, about how the goal is the same, and that we should love the Christians and try to have *Metta* for all Christians. *But I really felt that Buddhism was better*! So one day this was bothering me, because I thought: "What if somebody asks you- 'Which is the best religion?' -What would you say? Well, Buddhism, that's what I'd say" -and suddenly it became very clear that that was only an opinion and that opinions were not permanent conditions; they were not self and you did not need to have one or to believe in one. I did not have to be the authority, the one who says this is better than that. And I felt no longer any obligation to think about it or try to figure it out. It became clear that all I had to do was to be aware of the desire to know and the ability to say, "This is better than that."

One time several years ago I became obsessed with jealousy. As I was the senior monk I felt I had to set an example of perfect behaviour, and I began to feel jealous if other monks were praised. Somebody might say: "This monk is better than Sumedho," and I'd feel a tremendous sense of jealousy arise in my mind. It's a kind of competitiveness, feeling that you always have to hold your own in front of everybody else. But then I found that I did not like jealousy; it is a most unpleasant condition. So I tended to repress it. I would practice *Mudita*. When somebody would say: "That monk is better than Sumedho," I'd say to myself; "Isn't that wonderful, he's better than me", or, "Oh how glad I am for that person, he's better off than I am". *But I'd still feel jealous!* So I realised I had to look at the emotion and that the problem was that I was always trying to get rid of it. I decided to bring it up more; I started concentrating on

THE MONASTERY AS A TEACHER

1 -- Lay people and the Vihara.

.....Also, I would like to suggest that people coming here should, on occasion, bring candles, incense and flowers as an offering. This is a good tradition - to make an offering as part of our devotional practice as Buddhists, as an act of worship, of gratitude, of love towards the Teacher, the Buddha. The Buddha is the One Who Knows, the Wise One within us - but that's also just a conceptualisation. To use our bodies within conventions, in a harmonious and graceful way, inclining towards generosity - is in itself an act of giving. Is your attitude *"I come to the Vihara to get something"* or *"I come to the Vihara to give"* ? — to actually physically *give* something.

Bowing -- this is another tradition -- learning how to bow mindfully, putting one's head down, surrendering oneself physically, giving oneself in the act of bowing, instead of just saying *"I am not aggressive, I am not proud and arrogant"*. If you get proud that you bow so well, or if you start hating people that do not bow, then...! This is an act of devotion, and devotion is an opening of the heart, of the emotions rather than the intellect. *"How much do I gain from bowing?"* - you can try to figure out its advantages or disadvantages, whether it's the real Dhamma, or it's necessary or unnecessary. But any opinion and view that you have about it is just another opinion and view. Bowing is something that is *done* or not done - giving or not giving - but heedlessness is always this rationalisation, this wanting to criticise or analyse or find reasons for doing or not doing something. In our lives, if we live our lives in wisdom, then we do or not do. With awareness we know what to do - the generous, the beautiful, the kind, the spontaneous, good actions are done through awareness, through a seeing and understanding of time and place. Or there is awareness of not doing, of wrong impulses, selfish impulses, these we do not act upon.

Chanting - what is this? Is this a valuable thing, or is it useless? If you ever doubt about it - to do it or not do it - what goes on, do you know? Do you have to find reasons and justifications, do you have to be convinced? Or do you take some stand, saying *"I am not going to do it"* or *"I am going to do it"*. Some people are always saying *"Oh - chanting reminds me of all those awful things Roman Catholics used to do to me - blind devotion and rituals, rites and ceremonies."* This is taking a stand - can you mindfully participate in ceremony, or are you going to reject it because of a stand against it? Can you give yourself to a tradition, or are you going to say *"I'll only go so far, and then **stop**"*?

Like in the monastic life - can you give yourself to the monastic life, or are there going to be reservations - *"I'll go so far, then I don't know. In meditation, I'll go so far then 'maybe'"*? *"I want life on my terms and always with the bridges there so I can run back across them if I don't like what's ahead of me."* This is of course samsāra, heedless wandering.

In the practice of awareness, it is always the present moment, complete involvement, complete surrender, acceptance - and that is liberation. With the other, with the doubt, the rationalisations, justifications and reservations, then there is always a myriad complexities that are going to pull us this way and that and confuse us.

So I offer this for your reflection this evening.

2 -- an Anagarika Ordination

'Anagarika' means one who is leaving the home life for the homeless life - it implies relinquishment and renunciation as the homeless life is the life of the religious seeker, dedicating himself, or herself, solely to realising the Truth. Now a renunciate is someone who can take on the Precepts that limit and contain their energies, so that they're not finding themselves being pulled out this way and that, and they can concentrate their minds on the Truth - which we call inclining to *Nibbāna*, the unconditioned.

First of all, you did the traditional salutation in Pāli: *"Namo Tassa Bhagavato Arahato Sammāsambuddhassa."* - which is a way of reminding ourselves to be with that which is perfect, the purified, the truly compassionate, the enlightened. Then the taking of the Three Refuges - Buddha, Dhamma, Sangha - what do you really mean by taking refuge in Buddha? Recollect that a refuge is a place that you go to for safety; and that refuge of a Buddha means the refuge of wisdom. It's pointing to something very real, not something idealistic, or far and remote, but that which is wise within us, that which is wise in the universe, awake and clear. So, when you take Refuge in Buddha, it's not just an empty recitation, but a way for you to recollect, because we do forget and get caught up in our feelings and thoughts.

Then *"Dhammam Saranam Gacchāmi"* - the Dhamma is the Pali word for the Ultimate Reality, that which is ultimately true. We're taking Refuge in the immortal Truth, reminding ourselves to be with that which is true. *"Sangham Saranam Gacchāmi"* - taking Refuge in the Sangha, the virtuous ones, those who live by a code of nobility and virtue. This is the Bhikkhu-sangha, the Order of monks, but it also means that you are taking Refuge in a community, or with all human beings who are virtuous. Or you can look at it as taking Refuge in that in yourself which is virtuous, compassionate and good; and in the practical way of relating and living as a human being. Our way of relating to each other is through kindness, compassion and morality, rather than through exploitation and selfishness. In this way, you remind yourself to take Refuge in Sangha.

As a renunciate anagarika, you take the Eight Precepts.The first one is *pānātipātā* - to refrain from intentionally taking the life of any living creature. You have to learn to respect the life of living creatures, rather than just get rid of them for your own convenience; you have to be more considerate of even the most insignificant form of life, no matter how unpleasant it might be. *Pānātipātā* makes us more patient, more respectful towards the rights of all creatures on this earth, we're no longer looking at this earth as if *"...we're going to make this earth as we want it, so that it's convenient for us at the expense of everyone else."*

Then the *Adinnādānā* is refraining from taking things that do not belong to you, so that we train ourselves to respect that which belongs to others. The third Precept is the *Abrahmacariyā,* which means celibacy. This means total abstinence from any kind of intentional sexual behaviour. This is the way of a *Brahmacarin,* in which we relinquish sexual delight for the religious quest. In other words, we're taking the energy that goes out in sexuality up into the heart, the spiritual centre.

The fourth is *Musāvādā,* which means to refrain from lying, and to be more responsible for what one says - not using language for insulting others, for exaggeration or for gossip.

The fifth is *"Surāmeraya..."* - refraining from alcoholic drinks and drugs. As anagarikas, you're refraining from intentionally changing consciousness and recognising the way of mindfulness as one in which you open your minds and understand conditions, rather than try to get away from them by manipulating your minds.

The sixth Precept is a renunciate one of refraining from eating at the inappropriate time, so that we're not spending our whole day just indulging in eating food. The anagarika (and bhikkhu) can eat between dawn and noon - usually here we eat the one meal just before noon. In the winter, when it gets colder, we have rice gruel in the early morning, but the idea is to eat just what is necessary, rather than spend our time preparing and eating food. In ordinary life, one tends to munch on things all day long (at least I did) but here we limit, rather than just follow, our habits.

The long one* - which you did very well (congratulations!) - means you're no longer seeking distraction through entertainment. You're giving yourself up, when you get bored, or want some fun, to go to movies, to discos and so forth, by abstaining. However, this doesn't mean that we're *against* fun or entertainment, it means that we're simplifying our lives rather than seeking distraction through the sensual world. Now if we feel bored or weary, we move inward, towards the peace within. Actually, you begin to realise that true peace of mind is much more delightful than any kind of sensual pleasure, so that after a while the sense pleasures begin to seem not so enticing, as you begin to recognise the strength within yourself.

The last Precept is about sleeping. It is usually translated as not sleeping on high and luxurious beds, but can be regarded more as not seeking escape through sleeping all the time. There's that side of us that, whenever life becomes difficult, wants to sleep all the time, kind of eradicate ourselves through sleeping 14 hours a day - and of course that's possible if you have high, luxurious beds. But in the monastic life, we train ourselves to sleep on harder surfaces which are not the kind of places where you can spend hours lost in sleep. So you begin to develop your meditation and learn to limit the sleep to just what is necessary for the body, and know how much is an indulgence or an escape. Know yourself how to live with your body and mind in a way that is skilful.

Now these precepts are guidelines, they are not to be burdensome rules by which you feel guilt-ridden if you don't live up to the highest standard. This is a way of training - you're not expected to be perfect all at once - a way of guiding yourself towards recognising the

---

* Naccagitavaditavisukadassanamālāgandhavilepanadharanamandanavibhusanatthana veramani sikkhapadam samādiyami.

conditions of your mind; to recognise resistance, laziness, indulgence and the resentment of being restricted. You should want to see these things, so that you can release yourself from the burden of repression and the burden of indulgence and find the Middle Way.

This is a training period for one year, so that I expect you to stay at least one year under the discipline, and then decide whether you want to continue or not. This life is only valuable as long as you see its value. It's not a life of compulsion, it has to be voluntary, and the energy for it has to come from *your* mind. You can't expect somebody else to enlighten you. This is a very mature way of living in which you're developing from your heart, developing the effort from your *own* mind rather than just being conditioned into being Buddhists or monks. It's useless if you're just trying to rearrange your ways of life and thinking just to become something else. That's not liberation, is it?

Now as an anagarika, you no longer have a lot of choices and decisions to make about what to do, life here is much more one-pointed. So you have more time to watch. We live here under these principles so that we trust each other. We're not here to compete with each other, to see who's going to become 'anagarika of the year' - that would be working from the wrong attitude. Instead we learn to respect each other and have compassion for each other as human beings so that we're not being harsh or narrow-minded in regards to individual problems, abilities, or lack of abilities. We can't all be the same, but we can respect the differences.

So, even though we live in a community of many people, we allow the space of the mind, we forgive each other for the things we do wrong. Inevitably, living in a community with other beings means that there are going to be misunderstandings and conflict, but we work with that and with ourselves, rather than try to make the community fit what we would like it to be. This lesson is very important for a human being- to learn how to forgive – as many of the problems in the world arise because of a lack of forgiveness. Hundreds of years go by, and people are still talking about what somebody did to their relatives two hundred years ago! But as religious mendicants, we don't have to spend our time complaining, criticising members of the community, but rather learn how to let go of our particular views about them and give them the space to develop. Each of us has to develop from the position of what we are... recognising and realising, rather than becoming anything.

3 -- the first Bhikkhu Ordination

"Ehi bhikkhu!" - *"Come, bhikkhu!"* are the words from the Pali Canon that the Buddha used when he first ordained those interested in leading a life as a Buddhist monk (or *bhikkhu*). Those words were used over two millenia ago after the Blessed One turned the Wheel of the Law and began his ministry to aid beings lost in this world of change. The wheel has continued to turn, and on July 16th. we found ourselves in the tiny village of Chithurst in West Sussex, following a procedure that has evolved in the Theravāda tradition since the first invitation to Go Forth. That such an event took place says a great deal for the spiritual maturity, sincerity and generosity of the Buddhist community in Britain. The events that came to a culmination on this day once again show how perfect the natural unfolding of life can be.

Earlier this year, Ven. Sumedho Bhikkhu, the abbot and teacher at Chithurst Forest Monastery, was invited to Thailand by his Meditation Master, Ven. Ajahn Chah. Whilst there, he was given permission by the most senior of the bhikkhus of the Thai Sangha to perform the duties of an *Upajjhāya* (Preceptor) in Britain. Feeling it would be useful, he accepted this responsibility. However, one cannot just go out on a street corner or Hyde Park and ordain bhikkhus. A few important procedures have first to be completed. One of the most significant is establishing a boundary or *sīmā:* a specially defined area wherein acts of the Bhikkhu-Sangha may take place.

None of the bhikkhus at Chithurst had had much experience in performing this particular act of Sangha procedure. It is not something that often needs to take place in an ancient Buddhist country like Thailand. Although research into the correct procedure had been done, and a few likely locations in our woods were selected, there was a long pause when nothing much happened - except the day for ordination crept closer. It has been our experience that there is indeed a "time for all seasons" and there seemed to be a tacit understanding among the bhikkhus that, as yet, it wasn't the right time.

In the latter part of May, we had the good fortune to be visited by Ven. Ananda Maitreya Mahānāyaka. On the evening of June 2nd, after the recitation of the *Pātimokkha* (the Rules of the Discipline) we asked him about the procedures for establishing a *sīmā*.

"Oh it's very simple" he said. *"In Sri Lanka I have established over forty of them"*, and with his delightful smile asked, *"Shall we do it now?"*

We looked at each other - it was a short time before the evening meditation and after two weeks of almost continuous rain, it looked like rain again.

Sensing our hesitation, he said: *"Let us do it tomorrow then."*

It obviously was the right time. The local rain spirit went on holiday and June 3rd. broke bright, clear, sunny and warm. By the time the bell rang for the meal at 10:30 a.m., the *sīmā* at Chithurst Forest Monastery, the first in Britain, had been established. Out of gratitude, we have named the boundary the Ananda Maitreya Sīmā. To add to the beauty and auspiciousness of the day, an exquisitely carved figurine of Kuan Yin Bodhisattva was discovered in the garage of a local blacksmith. On hearing it identified as the Bodhisattva of Compassion, the owner generously offered the image to the monastery. She arrived at Chithurst just as the bhikkhus were acknowledging Ven. Sumedho as *Upajjhāya*. This acknowledgement was the first formal act of the Sangha in the newly-established *sīmā* boundary. It was a very special day.

The tempo of preparations began to quicken: the chanting of the bhikkhus-to-be and of the *Acariyas* for the ordination - Bhikkhus Ānando and Viradhammo – could be heard occasionally drifting through the house when there was a break in the din of construction work on the new shrine room. We rehearsed the ordination procedure, sewed the robes for the new monks, worked long hours on the new shrine room, and prayed for nice weather for the ordination day

There were over one hundred people at Chithurst Monastery on July 16th. for the ordination. This unusual gathering of people from many cultures occurred for a very special event - the going forth of three men into the life of a homeless one - a bhikkhu. Those who came sat around the *simā* on the grass or on chairs, and the occasion that so many had waited for, for such a long time, began very simply with a bow.

Ven. Ananda Maitreya insisted that Ven. Sumedho be the *Upajjhāya* for the ordination as he is the abbot and teacher at Chithurst. The actual ordination of the bhikkhus took only one hour, but for those wearing the robe for the first time this can be a traumatic experience. Everything feels like it's about to fall off, in front of one hundred people! To complicate matters, for some reason the robe material didn't shrink the 15% it was expected to. One had visions of new bhikkhus tripping on their much-too-long robes and sprawling head-first at the feet of Ven. Sumedho. Fortunately, nothing like that happened. The new bhikkhus, Jayamangalo, Sumano and Thitapañño, knew the correct responses, and without obstruction the *Acariyas* did their chanting, following the long-established tradition. Ven. Sumedho Bhikkhu acknowledged the completion of each ordination with a big smile, raising his hands in *anjali* as the new bhikkhu bowed to him for the first time.

It is recorded that in the middle of the third century B.C., the great king Asoka sent to Tissa, King of Ceylon, his son the Arahant Mahinda, to sow the seeds of the *Buddhasāsana* in that country. Around 1360 A.D., the then King of Thailand requested from Ceylon that bhikkhus be dispatched to preside over and validate ordinations in Thailand. In 1908, another Ananda Maitreya, the first English Bhikkhu, returned home from Sri lanka with aspirations for establishing the Order of Buddhist Monks here. In 1956, the English Sangha Trust was formed as a concrete step toward this same noble goal. And in 1981, with three of the most consistently supportive trustees present - Mr. Maurice Walshe, Mr. Geoffrey Beardsley and Mr. George Sharp - this goal was realised.

The ordination of the three bhikkhus was a joyous occasion. To actually see the *Buddhadhamma* transforming the worldly heart into one dedicated to the path of liberation is inspiring for all of us, and as a sign of the far-reaching significance of such a step, the Metta Sutta was recited at the completion of the ceremony, wishing well to the newly-ordained and dedicating the merit of the occasion to the liberation of all beings.

4--The Samana and Society

The teachings of the Buddha are the teachings that help us to understand ourselves, so we can use the teaching and do the work of the practice. Even though it's quite possible for us to figure it out on our own, I really doubt whether I would be able to do it, so I'm quite grateful to have an established form and convention to use as a guide in order to understand my emotions, memories and habits. Being committed to the convention of a samana means that it's something I give myself to voluntarily; it's something I feel grateful to and respect, so that I stay within the limitations that it places on me. 'Kataññū' - gratitude - arises in the mind. I remember the tremendous feeling of gratitude that arose towards Tan Ajahn Cha and Thai society when I realized that they had provided me with the occasion and the support to live like this and understand myself. When you realize the wonder of that you gladly live within the conventions, you want to perfect them and be worthy - as a way of offering back to those who have supported you. So one goes back into society, in order to be of service and give that occasion to others.

An alms-mendicant is one who gives the occasion for others to give alms. This is different from being a beggar going around scrounging off the neighbours...A lot of people think we're just a bunch of beggars. *'Why don't they go out and work? They probably laze around Chithurst House just waiting for someone to come along and feed them! Why don't they go out and get a job, do something important?'* But an alms-mendicant gives the occasion for others to give the alms that are necessary for existence - such as food, robes, shelter and medicine. You don't need very much and you have to live quite humbly and impeccably so you are worthy of alms. One reflects *'Am I worthy of this, have I been living honestly and rightly within the discipline?'* - because what people are giving to is not me as a personality, but the Sangha which lives following the teaching of the Buddha.

This monastery is dependent on alms, there are no fees for staying - it just depends on what people offer. If it was an institution based on fees, we wouldn't really be samanas anymore, we'd be businessmen, making a business out of teaching the Dhamma which has been freely given to us. A country like this is regarded as a benevolent and good country, but it has become too bureaucratic and too materialistic. Here in Europe, people have lost that 'kataññū', we've become very demanding, always complaining and wanting things better and better, even though we don't really need such a high standard. So as samanas, we give the occasion for people to give what they can, and that has a good effect on us as well as on the society. When you open up the opportunity in a society where people can give to things they respect and love, people get a lot of happiness and joy. But if we have a tyrannical society where we're constantly trying to squeeze everything out we can get, we have a miserable and depressed society. So in Britain now, we as monks and nuns make ourselves worthy of love and respect, people make offerings and more people experience the arising of faith. More people come and listen - they want to practise the Dhamma, they want to have the occasion to go forth and so it increases.....

Bhikkhus setting out for almsround in N.E. Thailand

'Patient endurance is the supreme austerity'

Dhammapada 184

PATIENCE

Patience is a virtue that is highly praised within Buddhist circles, but not considered so terribly important in the materialist world where efficiency and getting what we want instantly are far more desirable. With all the instant things that are produced now, as soon as we feel a desire, a need for something, we can get it quickly – and if we can't get it quickly we become very annoyed or upset and complain – "This country's going to the dogs." We hear that all the time, don't we, people complaining about everything? – because if people are going on strike, or aren't efficient enough, quick enough to satisfy our desires, we have to wait and patiently endure.

Notice in sitting, when pain arises in your body, how impatient you become, automatically trying to get away from pain. If you have a fever or become sick, notice how you resent the inconvenience, the annoyance of the body, and try to get well to get away from pain as soon as possible.

The virtue of patience is probably the most important one for us to consider at this time because if you don't have patience then of course spiritual development is an impossibility. So I might think – "I'll take the instant Zen practice, I don't want to be bothered with that Theravāda because it takes too long a time. I want to get enlightened *instantly*, quickly, so I don't have to wait around doing boring things, doing things that take time that I may not feel like doing. Maybe I can take a course or take a pill, have some kind of machine and get enlightened quickly." I remember when L.S.D. first became known, people were saying that it was the quick way to enlightenment– "You just swallow this tablet and you understand *everything!* You don't have to bother with ordination as a monk and have to sit around in a monastery – just take a pill and you'll be enlightened: go to the chemist or the dope-peddler and you don't have to commit yourself to anything.'' Wouldn't that be wonderful, if that was all one had to do? But then after a few trips on LSD, people began to realize that, somehow, the enlightening experience seemed to disappear and you were left in an even worse state than ever. No patience.

Now in a monastery the development of patience is a part of our way of life. In Thailand, in the forest monasteries of the North-East, you have a chance to become very patient, because there life is much less efficient and you have to endure. You have to endure through all kinds of unpleasant physical experiences– such as malarial fevers, and the hot season. The hot season in the North – East is one of the dreariest things I've ever experienced in my life. You wake up in the morning and think–'' Not another day''– everything seems so dreary. You think – ''Another hot day, an endless day of heat and mosquitoes and sweat''. A seemingly endless day, and one day after another. And then one reminds oneself–''What a wonderful opportunity for developing patience!'' You hear about modern American ways to enlightenment where you can get involved in the most interesting kinds of personal relationships and scientific machinery, doing absolutely fascinating things to each other, *and* get enlightened. And here you are, sitting in the hot season, a hot, dreary day, endless, in which one hour seems like an eternity. You think–''What am I doing here, I could be in California, having a fascinating life, doing fascinating things, getting enlightened quicker and more efficiently. California is much more advanced and with-it than the North-East of Thailand.'' And then you receive letters from impatient Americans who have gone around the world, visited all the Ajahns – ''What am I doing here, sweating through my robes, being bitten by mosquitoes?'' And then you think– ''I'm developing patience. If I just learn to be patient in this lifetime I've not wasted it– just to be a *little* more patient– it's good enough. I won't go to California, get caught up in those fascinating encounter groups, modern therapies and scientific experiments ...I'll just sit here and learn to be patient with a mosquito biting my arm ...learn to be patient with an endless, dreary hot season that seems to go on for ever."

Then I used to think – "My mind is too alert and bright, I've got so much restless movement in my mind." Because I always wanted to have an interesting personality, I trained myself in that direction and acquired all kinds of useless information and silly ideas, so I could be a charming, entertaining person. But it doesn't really count, it's useless in a monastery in North-East Thailand; that mental habit just goes around in your mind when you're alone with nobody to charm and nothing's fascinating anymore. Instead of becoming fascinating and charming– I could see there was no point in that – I started looking at the water buffaloes, and wondering what went on in their minds. A Thai water buffalo is one of the most stupid looking creatures in the whole world. It's a big, clumsy thing, and it has the dullest-looking face... "...That's what I need, to sit in my kuti, sweating through my robes, trying to imagine what a water buffalo is thinking." So I'd sit there and create in my mind an image of a water buffalo, becoming more stupid, more dull, more patient, and less of a fascinating and clever, interesting personality.

Just learning to be more patient with things as they are, with oneself – one's hang-ups, one's obsessive thoughts, restless mind...and with the way things are externally. Like here at Chithurst – how many of you are really *patient* with Chithurst? I hear some of you complaining that you have to work too hard, or there's not enough of *this*, or you want more time, or you want...there's too many people, not enough privacy...the mind goes on doesn't it? There's always some place, somewhere, that's better. But patience means that you endure through the way things are right now. How many of you would be willing to sit through a hot season in the North-East? Or endure through a year of having some tropical disease; patiently, without wanting to go home and have mother take care of you?

We still have the hope that eventually enlightenment will make us a more interesting, with-it person than an unenlightened being - if you could just get enlightened, you could surely increase the feeling of self-importance. But the Buddha wisdom is a very humbling wisdom, and it takes a great deal of patience to be wise like Buddha. Buddha wisdom isn't a particularly fascinating kind of wisdom – it's not like being a nuclear physicist, or a psychiatrist or a philosopher. Buddha wisdom is very humbling because it knows that whatever arises passes away and is not self. So it knows that *whatever* condition of the body and mind arises, it is conditioned, and whatever arises passes away. And it knows the unconditioned as the unconditioned.

But is knowing the unconditioned very interesting or fascinating? Try to think of knowing the unconditioned– would that be interesting? You might think– "I'd like to know God or Dhamma, it's going to be an incredibly fascinating thing to know, something blissful and ecstatic." So you look in your meditation for that kind of experience. You think that getting high is getting close. But the unconditioned is as interesting as the space in this room. The space in this room – is it very interesting to look at? It's not to me – the space in this room is like the space in the other room. The *things* in this room might be interesting or uninteresting or whatever – good, bad, beautiful, ugly – but the space...what is it? There is nothing you can really say or think about it, it has no quality except being spacious. And to be able to be really spacious, one has to be patient.

As there is nothing that one can grasp, one recognizes space only by not clinging to the objects in the room. When you let go, when you stop your absorptions, judgements, criticisms and evaluations of the beings and the things in the room, you begin to experience the space of it. But that takes a lot of patience and humility. With conceit and pride we can form all our opinions about whether we like the Buddha image or not, or the picture in the back, or the colour of the walls; whether we think the photograph of Ajahn Mun is an inspiring one, or the photograph of Ajahn Chah...but when we just sit here in the space...the body starts becoming painful, we become restless, or sleepy – *then* we endure, we watch and we listen. We listen to the mind, the complaining of the mind, the fears, the doubts and the worries – not in order to come up with some fascinating, interesting conclusions about ourselves as *being* anything, but just as a mere recognition, a bare recognition that all that arises, passes away. Buddha wisdom is just that much – knowing the conditioned as the conditioned and the unconditioned as the unconditioned.

Buddhas rest in the unconditioned, and no longer, unless it's necessary, seek absorption into anything. They are no longer deluded by any conditions, and they incline to the unconditioned, the spaciousness, the emptiness, rather than towards the changing conditions within the space.

In your meditation now, as you incline towards the emptiness of the mind, towards the spaciousness of the mind, your habitual grasping, fascination, revulsions, fears, doubts and worries about the conditions lessen. You begin to recognize they're just things that come and go; they're not self, nothing to get excited about or depressed about, they are as they are. We can allow conditions to be just as they are, because they come and they go – their nature is to go away, so we don't have to make them go away. We're free and patient and enduring enough to allow things to take their natural course. In this way, we liberate ourselves from struggle, strife, and the confusion of an ignorant mind that has to spend all its time evaluating and discriminating, trying to hold onto something, trying to get rid of something.

So reflect on what I've said, and have all the time in the world to endure the unendurable. What seems to be unendurable is endurable if you are patient...be patient with others, and with the world as it is, rather than always dwelling on what's wrong with it and how you'd like it to be if you had your way. Remember the world happens to be as it is, and right now that's the only way it can be. The only thing we can do is be patient with it. It doesn't mean that we approve or like it any the more, it means we can exist in it peacefully rather than complaining, rebelling and causing more frictions and confusion; than adding to the confusion through believing in our own confusion.

Offering food to the monks on their almsround

For hatred is never appeased
by hatred in this world;
only by non-aversion
is aversion appeased.
This is the eternal law.

Dhammapada 5

"THE PRACTICE OF METTĀ"

This evening I would like to talk about the practice of Mettā, a meditation which most people will find very useful. The concept of Mettā is generally translated as "loving kindness". This may be too big a word because we tend to think of "loving kindness" as grand and wonderful and sometimes we cannot generate that kind of love for everything.

The English word "love" is often misused. We say "I love to eat fish and chips", when what we mean is "I like to eat fish and chips". The Christians talk about "Christian love", this means the love of your enemies, it does not mean liking them. How can you like your enemies? We can, however, love them, which means that we will not do anything to harm them. We will not dwell in aversion on them. You can be kind to your enemies, kind towards people who are not very nice to you, who insult you and wish you harm. They may be unpleasant people whom you cannot like, but can love. You can love them in the sense of not doing anything to harm them, not being vindictive, not dwelling in aversion on them. Mettā is not a kind of superman's love - it is the very ordinary ability to just be kind and not dwell in aversion on something or someone.

If right now, a man walked into this room - drunk, ugly, diseased, stinking, cursing and swearing, with warts all over his face - we could not even consider liking him, but we can be kind. We would not have to punch him in the nose, curse him and force him out of the room. We could invite him in and give him a cup of tea. We can be kind, we can do something for someone who is repulsive and disgusting in some way. When we think to ourselves "I can't stand that man, get him out of here, he is disgusting", it becomes impossible to be kind and we are creating suffering around what is unpleasant to us.

There is a great lack of Mettā in the world today, because we have overdeveloped our critical faculties. We constantly analyse and criticise. We dwell on what is wrong with ourselves, with others, with the society we live in. Mettā, however, means not dwelling in aversion, being kind and patient, even towards that which is bad, evil, foul or terrible. It is easy to be kind towards nice animals like little kittens and puppies. It is easy to be kind towards people we like, towards sweet little children, especially when they are not ours. It is easy to be kind to old ladies and old men when we do not have to live with them. It is easy to be kind to that which agrees with us politically and philosophically and which does not threaten us in any way. It is much more difficult to be kind to that which we don't like, which threatens us or which disgusts us. That takes much more endurance.

First we have to start with ourselves. So, in traditional Buddhist style, we always start the practice of Mettā by having Mettā for ourselves. This does not mean we say "I really love myself, I really like me". When we practise Mettā towards ourselves, we do not dwell in aversion on ourselves any more. We extend kindness towards ourselves, towards conditions of body and mind. We extend kindness and patience even towards faults and failings, towards bad thoughts, moods, anger, greed, fears, doubts, jealousies, delusions - all that we may not like about ourselves.

When I first went to England, I asked the Buddhist people there whether they did the practice of Mettā. They said "No, can't stand it: It's so false. We're supposed to go around saying 'I like myself, I love myself, may I be happy'. It's so soppy, wet, foolish, I don't really feel it. It seems so false and superficial." On that level it sounded a bit silly to me too, until I realised that it wasn't taught in the right way and had become sentimental, a cosmetic covering up of things. The people of England could not go along with it, they would rather sit and analyse themselves, look at their faults and exaggerate them out of all proportion. They thought they were being honest with themselves.

When we practice Mettā towards ourselves, we stop trying to find all our weaknesses, faults and imperfections. Usually when you have a bad mood or start to feel depressed, you think "Here I go again, I'm worthless". When this happens, have Mettā for the depression itself. Don't make a bad thing out of it, don't complicate it, be at peace with it. Peacefully co-exist with the depressions, fears, doubts, anger or jealousy. Don't create anything around them with aversion.

Last year a woman came to ask me about depression, she said "I suffer from depression on occasions. I know it's bad, I know I shouldn't and I want to know what to do about it. I really don't want it, I want to get rid of it, what do you suggest?" Now what is wrong with depression? You expect that you should never feel depressed because of an idea that there's something wrong with you for being that way. Sometimes life just isn't very pleasant, it can be downright depressing. You can't expect life to be always pleasant, inspiring and wonderful.

I know how depression arises when there are unhappy things and unpleasant scenes around, I saw a lot of it during my first year in England. After living in a warm, sunny country like Thailand, where the people have great respect for the monks, always addressing you as "Venerable Sir", giving you things and treating you as if you are terribly important, I found that in England people treat you (the monks) as if you are crazy. London isn't sunny and smiling, it can be drizzling and cold and people are not interested in you at all. They look at you and just turn away without giving you a smile. In Thailand, life was so simple and easy for a Buddhist monk. We had nice forest monasteries in natural surroundings and our own little huts amongst the trees. In London we were cooped up in a grotty little house day after day, kept indoors by the drizzling rain and cold. So all the monks began to feel depression and negativity. We would just go through the motions of being monks. We would get up at 4.00 a.m., make it to the shrine room to do a little chanting, get that over with and then sit in meditation for a while, drink tea, go out for a walk - just going through the motions. We weren't putting any energy into anything we were doing, we were getting caught up in that which was depressing. There was also a lot of friction, a lot of problems in the group which had invited us to England, a lot of personality clashes and misunderstandings. When I reflected on it, I began to see that what I was doing was getting caught in the unpleasant things that were happening around me, I was creating negative feelings around that. I was wishing I was back in Thailand, wishing the unpleasant things would go away, wishing it wouldn't be the way it was, worrying about people and wishing they were otherwise.

I began to realise that I was dwelling in aversion on the unpleasant things around me. There were a lot of unpleasant things happening and I was creating aversion around it all. I was complicating it all in my mind so I was suffering for it. We decided to put effort into just being there; we stopped complaining, we stopped demanding or even thinking and wishing about being somewhere else. We began to put energy into our practice, getting up early, doing exercises to keep warm and we began to feel much better. Everything around us was the same, but we learned not to create problems within overselves over those difficulties.

When you have high expectations for yourself, thinking you have to be Superman or Wonderwoman, then of course you dont't have much Mettā, because only very seldom can we live up to such a high standard. You become doubtful of yourself: "Maybe I'm not good enough". By practicing Mettā towards ourselves we can stop doing that. We begin to forgive ourselves for making mistakes, for giving in to weaknesses. It doesn't mean that you rationalise things away, but rather that you do not go on creating problems or dwelling in aversion on the faults you have and the mistakes you have made.

So by applying the practice of Mettā inwardly, we can become a lot more peaceful within ourselves, with the conditions of our minds and bodies. We become more mindful and aware, more awake to the way things are. Wisdom begins to arise and we can see how we create unnecessary problems all the time by just following the momentum of habit.

Mettā means a little more than just kindness. It is a penetrating kindness, an awareness - kind awareness. Mettā means we can co-exist peacefully in a kindly way with the sentient beings within us and with beings outside. It does not mean liking, does it? Some people go to that extreme. They say "I love my weaknesses because that's really me. I wouldn't be me if I didn't have my wonderful weaknesses". That's silly. Mettā is being patient, being able to co-exist with, rather than trying to annihilate the pests of our minds.

Our society is very much one that annihilates pests both inwardly and outwardly, wanting to create an environment where there are no pests. I hear monks say "I can't meditate because there are too many mosquitos, if only we could get rid of them." Even though you can never really like mosquitos, you can have Mettā for them, respecting their right to exist and not getting caught up in resentment at their presence. Similarly, if I can have Mettā for the depressed mood at the moment and allow it to be there, recognising it and not demanding that it not be there, it will go. Feelings like these arise naturally and go away. We make them stay longer because we want them to go all the time. The struggle of trying to get rid of something we do not like seems to make it stay longer than it would otherwise.

The more we try to control nature, manipulate it according to our greed and desire, the more we end up polluting the whole earth. People are getting really worried now because we can see so much pollution from all the chemicals and pesticides that we use to try to get rid of the things in nature that we don't want. When we try to annihilate the pests in our mind we end up with pollution too - we have nervous breakdowns and then the pests come back stronger than ever.

Our modern society does not encourage much Mettā towards the old, the sick and the dying. Our society is very much oriented towards youth and vigour, being fast and staying young for as long as possible. When you get old, you're kind of useless, you can't do anything very well, you're slow, you're no longer attractive, so people don't really want to know you. Many old people feel they have no place in society. They get old and are cast aside as useless people. Our society treats the intellectually handicapped and the mentally ill in the same way. We try to keep them away so that we don't have to look at them and know they're around. Trying to ignore the facts of life such as death, infirmity and old age results in an increasing amount of mental illness, mental breakdowns and alcoholism.

In schools in the United States, we tried to get all the intelligent students with high I.Q.s together in one class and the slow and dumb ones in another. We did not want the intelligent students to be slowed down by the halting progress of the dumb ones. I think the most important thing the intelligent can learn is to be kind and patient towards those who are not as intelligent or quick as they are.

When we are forced to compete with our own kind, life becomes hectic and frustrating. Kindness, patience and compassion are much more helpful qualities for knowing how to live in the world than getting first prize and coming first in the class. Feeling that we always have to strive and compete to survive makes us neurotic and miserable. Those who can't compete feel inferior and just drop out. We have frustration and unfulfillment among the gifted as well as the not so gifted because Mettā has never been considered important. When we practice Mettā we begin to be willing to learn from termites and ants, from people who are slow, from the old, sick and dying. We become willing to take time out to take care of somebody who is ill and that takes patience doesn't it? we become willing to take time out of our busy lives to help and be with somebody who is dying. We become willing to try to contemplate and understand dying. This is the direction we must take to create a really humane and good society.

Before we can start making great changes in society, we have to start with ourselves, having Mettā for the conditions of our minds and bodies. We can have Mettā for the disease when we are ill. It does not mean that we are going to help the disease stay for a long time or that we should not have an injection of penicillin because we are having Mettā for the little germs infecting us. It means not dwelling in aversion on the discomfort and the weakness of our bodies when they are ill. We can learn to meditate on the fevers, fatigue, bodily pain and aches that we all experience. We don't have to like them, all we need to do is to take the time to endure them and try to understand them rather than just resenting them. When we do not have Mettā we just tend to react to those conditions with a desire to annihilate and the desire to annihilate always takes us to despair. We keep on re-creating all the conditions for despair in our minds when we just try to annihilate all that we do not like and do not want.

Living in a Buddhist monastery is good training for learning to live with people. As a layman I had some control over whom I associated with. keeping close to certain friends whom I liked to be with and staying away from anyone I did not like. But in the monastery we did not have any choice, we had to live with whoever was there, whether you liked them or not. So sometimes you had to live with people whom you did not like or whom you found irritating and annoying. That was good for me because I began to understand people whom I would never have taken the time to understand otherwise. If I had had a choice, I would not have lived with some of the people, but as that choice was not available I learned to be more sensitive and open. I learned to have Mettā and allow people to be as they are rather than always trying to force them to change, forcing them to be as I would like them to be or trying to get rid of them.

Wisdom arises when we begin to accept all the different "beings" both within ourselves and outside, rather than always trying to manipulate things so that it is convenient and pleasant for us all the time, so that we do not have to be confronted with irritating and troublesome people and situations. Let's face it, the world is an irritating place!

From my own experience I learned how frustrating life is when I have ideas of how I want it to be. So I began to look at my own suffering rather than just trying to control everything according to my desires. Instead of making requests and demands or trying to control everything, I began to flow with life, and that was much easier in the long run than all the manipulation that I used to do. We can still be fully aware of the imperfections and not dismiss them or be irresponsible; the practice of Mettā means we are not creating problems around it by dwelling in aversion. We can allow ourselves to flow with life.

Our experience of life sometimes isn't very pleasant, enjoyable or beautiful, at other times it's all of these. That's the way life is. The wise person can always learn from both extremes without attaching to either and not creating problems but peacefully co-existing with all conditions.

Ordination Ceremony *(Upasampadā)* — Chithurst Monastery

'...he, refraining from such views, grasps at nothing in the world; and not grasping, he trembles not; and trembling not, he by himself attains to perfect peace. And he knows that rebirth is at an end, that the higher life has been fulfilled, that what had to be done has been accomplished, and that there is no more becoming.'

Dīgha Nikāya XV—68

KAMMA AND REBIRTH

Kamma is a subject people like to talk about; to speculate about with opinions and views concerning what we were in the past and what might become of us in the future; about how our *kamma* affects someone else's and so forth. What I try to do is point out how to use these. *Kamma* and rebirth are words; they're only concepts that point to something that we can watch. It's not a matter of believing in *kamma* or disbelieving, but of knowing what it really *is*.

Kamma actually means to *do,* and we can observe it by being aware of what we are conscious of in the moment. Whatever it is: whatever feeling or sensation, thought or memory, pleasant or unpleasant, it's *kamma* – something moving from its birth to its death. Now this you can see directly, but it's so simple that, of course, we would like to speculate about it: why do we have the *kamma* we do have, what happens if we aren't enlightened, will we be born in a higher realm if we practise hard, or will the *kamma* from previous lives overwhelm us? Or we speculate about re-birth: what is it that carries on from one life to the next if there's no soul? If everything's *anattā,* how can I have been something in a previous life and have some essence that is born again?

But if you watch the way things operate independently of yourself, you begin to understand that re-birth is nothing more than desire seeking some object to absorb into which will allow it to arise again. This is the habit of the heedless mind. When you get hungry, because of the way you've been conditioned, you go out and get something to eat. Now that's an actual re-birth: seeking something, being absorbed into that very thing itself. Re-birth is going on throughout the day and night, because when you get tired of being reborn you annihilate yourself in sleep. There's nothing more to it than that. It's what you can see. It's not a theory but a way of examining and observing kammic actions.

"Do good and you'll receive good; do bad and you'll receive bad." We worry: "I've done so many bad things in the past; what kind of result will I get from all that?" Well, all you can know is that what you've done in the past is a memory now. The most awful, disgusting thing that you've ever done, that you wouldn't want anyone to know about; the one that, whenever anybody talks about *kamma* and re-birth, makes you think: "I'm really going to get it for having done that" – that is a memory, and that memory is the kammic result. The additions to that like fearing, worrying and speculating – these are the kammic results of unenlightened behaviour. What you do, you remember; it's as simple as that. If you do something kind, generous or compassionate, the memory makes you feel happy; and if you do something mean and nasty, you have to remember *that*. You try to repress it, run away from it, get caught up in all kinds of frantic behaviour – that's the kammic result.

Kamma will cease through recognition. In mindfulness, you're allowing kammic formations to cease rather than recreating them, or annihilating them and recreating them. It's important to recollect that whatever you create you destroy, and what you annihilate you create – one conditions the other, just as the inhalation conditions the exhalation. One is the kammic result of the other. Death is the kammic result of birth, and all we *can* know about that which is born and dies is that it is a condition and not self. No matter what the memory might be, it's not self. If you have the memory of murdering 999 people – that's just a horrendous memory now. Maybe you think: "That's getting off too easy; somebody who's killed 999 people should suffer a long time and be punished and tormented!" But it's not necessary that we go to any lengths to punish anyone because the punishment is the memory. As long as *we* remain ignorant, unenlightened, selfish beings, then we tend to create more kammic cycles. Our lack of forgiveness, lack of compassion, of trying to get even with "those evil criminals" – that's our *kamma:* we have the kammic result of the miserable state of hatred.

As Buddhists, we take refuge in the Ultimate Truth, and in the

Buddha, Dhamma and Sangha as conventional forms. This means that we have confidence in the Ultimate Truth, in the uncreated and the un-conditioned, not in conceiving but in recognising conditions as conditions and allowing kammic formations to cease. We just keep recognizing conditions instead of being fascinated and creating more *kamma* around those conditions through fear, envy, greed and hatred. This is a gentle recognition that kammic formations are what we are not. There's nothing we can say about what we are because in Ultimate Truth there are no beings, nobody is ever born or dies.

Our path of practice is to do good, to refrain from doing evil with body and speech, and to be mindful. Don't create complexities around it, or seek perfection in the realm of the senses. Learn to serve and help each other. Take refuge in Sangha by being confident of your intentions to be enlightened, to do good, to refrain from doing evil. Maybe you'll fail sometimes but that's not your intention – and always allow others to fail. We may have ideas and opinions about each other, but give each other space to be imperfect rather than demand that everyone be perfect in order not to upset you. That's very selfish, isn't it? But that's what we do, pick and choose: "These are the ones we want; these are the ones we don't want... These are worthy; these are unworthy... These are the ones that are really trying; these are the ones that aren't..."

Now, for peace of mind, when somebody does something wrong, recognize it as a kammic formation. To think, "How dare they do that; how dare they say that; how many years have I been teaching now, giving myself up for the welfare of all sentient beings and I don't get any thanks for it...!" – that's an unpleasant mental state. That's the result of wanting everybody else never to fail me, to always live up to my expectations, or at least to cause me no problems. Of wanting people to be other than they are. But if I don't expect you to *be* anything, I don't *create* anyone in my mind. If I think, "That's so-and-so, who did *this,* and then he did *that!*", then I'm creating a person out of kammic conditions and I suffer accordingly with an unpleasant memory every time I see you. Now, if you're ignorant and do that to me, and I do it back to you again, then we just reinforce each other's bad habits.

We break these habits by recognizing them, by letting go of our grudges and memories, and by not creating thoughts around the *vipāka**, the conditions of the moment. By being mindful we free ourselves from the burden of birth and death, the habitually recreating pattern of *kamma* and re-birth. We recognise the boring, habitual re-creations of unsatisfactoriness, the obsessions with worry, doubt, fear, greed, hatred and delusion in all its forms. When we're mindful, there's no attachment to ideas and memories of self, and creativity is spontaneous. There's no-one who loves or is loved; there's no personal being created. In this way we find the real expression of kindness, compassion, joy and equanimity that is always fresh, always kind, patient and ever forgiving of oneself and others.

---

* Just as 'kamma' is the cause, 'vipāka' is the effect in the kammic process.

A meditation hut *(kuti)* in Hammer Wood.

'And gladness springs up within him on his realising that, and joy arises to him thus gladdened, and so rejoicing all his frame becomes at ease, and being thus at ease he is filled with a sense of peace, and in that peace his heart is stayed.'

Digha Nikáya II -- 73

REALIZING THE MIND

In giving talks on meditation, one is really saying the same things over and over, but it's necessary to do so because we keep forgetting over and over and have to keep being reminded. Remember : what we remember we forget ; if you have nothing to remember, you have nothing to forget ; so in meditation we are moving towards where there is nothing to remember and nothing to forget. Which doesn't mean 'nothing', but a centreing : a realization of the ultimate reality, of that which is not conditioned.

Realization is not gaining, is it? You don't 'gain' realization. You realize something which you have all the time yet which you never notice. Meditation is not a gaining process either. We are not here to make ourselves into Buddhas or *Bodhisattvas* or *Arahants* or anything else, nor to try to just condition our minds into being Buddhist. You might think you just have to have a religious brainwash, throw away all your Christian habits and simply train yourself to think like a Buddhist – wear the robe, try to look like a Buddha image, use all these *Pali* words and call ourselves 'Buddhists'. Another costume isn't it? Another act ; another role to play. So the purpose of our meditation is not to become 'Buddhists' either.

Realization is what? Think, the word 'real' : realizing, recognizing, knowing, direct knowledge of ultimate truth...Now what do we mean by ultimate truth? We can say, 'Ultimate Truth', *'Dharma'*; we can use the *Pāli* word, *Dhamma,* or the Sanskrit word, *'Dharma';* we can say, 'The Absolute'; we can say 'God'. Whatever word one happens to be conditioned with is the word which one prefers. 'Ultimate Truth' might sound a bit intellectual or not have the pull of the heartstrings that 'God' has, but we're not quibbling about terminology anymore.

We don't care exactly what word we use. We're not here trying to find the perfect word to describe something which doesn't need any description, cannot REALLY be described but can only be realized. We just do the best we can with whatever language we happen to have, because the point is not to decide which terminology is the most accurate but to get beyond the term to the actual realization! Of 'Ultimate Reality' or 'God' or 'The Absolute' or whatever!

On the level of religious symbolism and convention we can spend our time quibbling about the 'Buddhist view', 'Buddhist *Dhamma*', 'Christian God', get caught up in all kinds of interesting little differences and comparisons. For what? For something one hasn't realized yet, like the blind men describing the elephant. It's not that we need to have the perfect word or the most accurate description but to have the intention to get to the reality – have that one-pointed intention, that sincerity, that kind of earnestness that takes you to the realization of truth, *Dhamma.* So, if it's already here now, then you don't have to go around looking for it. They have all these nice stories about religious pilgrims, religious seekers going off to the Himalayas looking for some saint living in a cave or looking for some mystic, some hermit, some *arahant,* who lives off in some remote valley or mountain crag, who knows the truth. We must find that person because he is our teacher and he is going to give us that truth. We have romantic visions of ourselves suddenly meeting our teacher: we climb up some remote Himalayan mountain crag, breathing hard, the air getting thinner – and he's standing there with eyes bright, radiant with love, saying: *"At last you've come!".* We can, on that fictional level, create interesting visions and fairy-tales about religious seeking; but the journey is an inward one. So how do we go inward, journey inside ourselves?

We start looking for something, the ultimate reality, as something we're going to find by looking within. So we think: "Meditation is the way. I don't need to go to India. That's foolish rubbish; I don't need to go to the Himalayan mountains. I can just meditate and find the truth within myself". And that's a very good idea – but what is the truth and what are you looking for?

Is the truth something?

Does it have a quality that we would be able to recognize?

Now, the religious journey is what we call "inclining to *Nibbāna*", turning away, inclining away from the sensory world to the unconditioned; so it's a very subtle kind of journey. It's not something you can do just as an act of will – you can't just say, "I'm going to realize the truth", and do it. "I'm going to get rid of all my defilements, hindrances; get rid of lust, hatred, all my weaknesses and I'm going to get there!!". People who do that usually go crazy. One man I met years ago who had been a *bhikkhu* was in a mental hospital. This man had been a '*maha*', meaning he had taken all the *Pali* examinations. He went off to a mountain top, went into his little hut and said, "I'm not coming out until I'm perfectly enlightened" – and came out stark raving mad! So if it's just an act of will and ego then, of course, it takes you to madness. You keep bashing away, knocking about in your mind. With the ego you just get caught in a trap. It seems a web of madness, hard to see beyond or ever extricate yourself from. So meditation isn't something we do to attain or achieve or get rid of anything, but to realize.

So what can we realize now? What can we realize right now?

"Well I've been looking for the Ultimate Reality the whole time I've been sitting here and I can't find it".

What can you realize or know now, whatever it is, whatever your state of mind is; whether you're agitated, if you're having bad thoughts; if you're angry, if you're upset, bored, frightened, doubtful, uncertain, or whatever? *You can recognize that that's what is going on now.* It's a realization that now there is THIS condition: of fear, doubt, worry, some kind of desire, and that it is a changing thing.

If you're frightened of something, try to hold onto that fear, make it stay so that it becomes a permanent condition in your mind. See how long you can stay frightened; see if fear is the ultimate reality, is God. Is fear God, the Ultimate Truth? You can see fear. When I'm frightened I know it. There's fear, but also, when I truly realize there's fear, its power to delude me diminishes. Fear only has power if I keep giving it the power; and how does fear have power? By deluding us, by making it seem more than what it is. Fear presents itself in a big way and we react: we run away, and then it gains power over us. That's how to feed the fear demon: by reacting in the way that it wants you to. The fear demon comes – ferocious, nasty – looking demon – scowls and frowns, shows its fangs and you go, *"Ooh! Help!!"*, and run away. Then that demon thinks. *"This really is a sucker!"*.

If you realize the demon, you recognize that the demon is a condition; nothing more than that. No matter how ferocious or nasty it might appear, it's nothing really. Simply recognize it as a condition that looks fierce and nasty. Fear, the feeling of fear – you begin to recognize that fear is just an illusion of the mind – conditioned. Desire, any form of desire, is the same way – it has its appearance, it seems to be more than what it really is. Meditation is breaking down, breaking through the illusion of the way things seem to be by recognizing, realizing conditions as they are: as changing, as unsatisfactory and as not having any personal quality, not any personal self or soul, as just something that comes and goes, changes. You begin to stand back, you feel a space, a gap in yourself. After a while things that used to completely overwhelm and demolish you seem more distant; you have a way of looking at them as if they were something separate rather than what you are: 'what *I* am'.

Meditation is a constant realizing. Realizing the conditions of the mind as just that: as conditions of the mind. Ignorant people do not understand this. They think the conditions of mind are themselves, or they think they shouldn't have certain conditions and that they should have other kinds of conditions. If you are a very idealistic person you would like to be good, saintly, intelligent, noble, courageous, the finest quality of human being. "That's what I want to be. I want to be a very noble and fine person". Well, that's all very good, you have this ideal: *"That's what I'd like to be;"* 'the noble heart', 'the courageous man', 'the gentle, compassionate woman'; all these wonderful ideals, but then you have to face the realities of daily life. We find ourselves being caught up in getting angry, getting upset, jealous, greedy, thinking all kinds of un- pleasant things about people who we know, thoughts and feelings that if we were the perfect human beings we would like to be we would never think or feel. So then we start thinking: *"I am so far removed from that ideal human being, that wonderful man, that perfect woman, that I'm a hopeless, useless, worthless BUM!"*. Why? Because the conditions of your mind are not always fitting the ideal; sometimes you might be very courageous, very noble-hearted. At certain moments we find ourselves doing the most wonderful things, acting in a most courageous way. But at other times the opposite is the case. We wonder, *"How do such ugly thoughts come into my mind? If I were really good I would never have such evil thoughts or feelings"*.

Now, what we can realize, without trying to become anything, is that these conditions are just that. Whether they are noble, brave and courageous, or weak, wishy-washy, ignoble and stupid, they are still only conditions dependent on all kinds of factors that we can't predict or control. Begin to realize that on the conditional level of *samsara* everything is affecting everything. There's no way that we can say, "I am going to isolate myself completely from everything so that nothing is affecting me", because everything is affecting everything all the time. So on the conditioned level there's nothing much we can do except recognize, realize; although we do have a choice. We can use our bodies for good action rather than evil; that's where the choice comes. If you're mindful and wise then you skillfully use your body and speech, that which goes out, relates to other beings and to the earth you live on – you use it skillfully, for that which is kind, compassionate, charitable, moral.

What goes on in the mind could be anything: maybe the desire to kill somebody. But that is something you don't act upon. You just recognize. You can recognize it's only a condition and not a 'self', not a personal problem. Now have any of you ever had any murderous impulses? Wanting to kill somebody? I have. I can understand murder. I never murdered anybody, never came close, but I have certainly had murderous thoughts. So where do those come from? Is there something really rotten inside me that I should start worrying about, or is it just the natural tendency of a mind – that when you feel totally repelled and averse to something you try to annihilate it? That's natural enough. Murder is a part of nature; it goes on all the time. Animals murder each other. Just listen some nights in the forest. You hear murders going on all the time: rabbits screaming as foxes grab their throats. Murder is a natural inclination, it's nothing abnormal; but for the moral, responsible human being, the religious seeker, we might have murderous impulses but we do not act on them. Instead, we fully recognize these impulses as that: as impulses, as conditions. What I mean by recognizing is the realization, "They are just that"; not creating a problem, not making it complicated by saying, "We shouldn't have such impulses", or "I am a bad and evil man because such an impulse came through my mind", and so start creating a neurosis around it. Just that clear realization of it as it really is, because that's what we can know directly, without speculation, without belief.

So that's a realization isn't it? Realizing the conditioned as the conditioned.

Now as we are more at ease with the conditioned, rather than deluded, helplessly reacting to conditions, absorbed into them, rejecting or annihilating them, we begin to be aware of the unconditioned, the space of the mind. You think that conditions are everything. Conditions have to come from something, don't they? Since they are impermanent, where do they come from and what do they disappear into? As you watch you begin to feel or experience the emptiness or the wholeness or the unconditioned – whatever word you use isn't quite it. We say 'the unconditioned', that which is not born, does not die.

So that's realization too, for those of you who have realized that. That's reality. The conditioned is reality, but the quality or appearance of a condition is not reality, ultimate reality. It's only a conventional appearance, the way things seem to be on a habitual, conventional level. Buddhist meditation is the practice of being awakened, being Buddha by recognizing, by realizing the way things REALLY are as you experience directly whatever it is: pain in your kness, a feeling of happiness, any sensation, thought, memory or emptiness; without grasping, without selecting, picking or choosing. We develop the equanimous heart, the mind that is balanced, full, complete and whole, seeing things as they really are, no longer deluded by any thing,by no-thing or by nothing.

When I talk about realization, do you see what I mean? It's a realizing. It's not a searching for 'God' or 'Ultimate Truth' as if it were some 'thing'. Look at the word itself. You say "God", and it makes it sound like some 'thing' doesn't it? It does to me anyway: the word 'God' sounds like something, somebody, as if it were a kind of condition. So, at the intellectual level, you can only go so far on the religious path, only as far as a belief. If you believe in words or ideas but never get beyond that, you're still caught in an attachment to an idea about the truth rather than KNOWING the truth. That's why the Buddha did not teach any kind of doctrine or belief system. I hear Buddhists say, "Buddhists don't believe in God and we don't believe in the soul ; if you're a real Buddhist, you don't have any of that stuff, souls and gods ; soulless and godless is what we are". But that's an annihilationist teaching, isn't it? That's pure annihilationism. Disbelieving in God and a soul is just the opposite of the other, of believing; it's not a realizing of truth. It's only the believing of a negation rather than the believing of an affirmation. I meet Buddhists who were Christians at one time and somehow they have been very disillusioned and they have become very anti-Christian. Because of that they use Buddhism as a justification. They put down Christianity and they think, "Those Christians believe in God. They're stupid. But we don't. And those Christians believe in an eternal soul, but we don't ; we don't believe in that stuff. We believe in *Anattā*, no soul!" But that is not what the Buddha was teaching. That is also a trap of the mind, limited, deluding us.

Realization is when you find out and know directly. It's not an affirmation, saying what *Dhamma* or the truth is, saying "It's male", or "The *Dhamma* is a man", or "The *Dhamma* is a patriarchal figure", "The *Dhamma* is nothing", "The *Dhamma* is an impersonal essence" or "The *Dhamma* is the essence of everything", "The *Dhamma* is everything and all"; getting into these philosophical positions, intellectual positions that people like to take about things they haven't realized yet. We're not trying to define that which is indefinable but to KNOW, to realize that which is beyond definition, beyond limitation.

So our Buddhist practice is just that. We have to keep reminding ourselves because the force of habit is so strong – we so easily absorb into our thoughts and memories; so easily absorb into habits of looking for something or trying to get rid of something; so easily believe all the opinions and views we have about ourselves and others and the world we live in. We so easily believe because some of our opinions and views are so sensible, so rational, so practical, reasonable, intelligent, brilliant -"The brilliant views and opinions that I have". We are not trying to say that you shouldn't have brilliant views and opinions either. It's all right to have brilliant views and opinions, as long as you recognize that that's what they are. They are impermanent conditions of mind: don't exaggerate their importance. Also don't feel bad if you're not very intelligent and have really stupid views and opinions; don't worry about it. Because that is just the same as the other as far as we're concerned. A realization rather than an affirmation or a negation.

In this way of realizing is what we call The Middle Way. It's mindfulness, meaning the mind is open, full, complete. You're no longer taking just a fragment and attaching, obsessing yourself with one little bitty condition, saying "This little bitty condition, this tiny little insignificant opinion that I have is the Ultimate Reality".

What I am presenting this evening, (you've heard it over and over) is to remind you, for you to reflect on, to keep recognizing, realizing. The little things in daily life, work with them, begin to really watch. If you're looking for something, if you hate authority, if some monk says, "Do this, do the dishes", and you feel resentment or anger – someone telling you to do something – that's a condition of mind! Keep recollecting rather than getting caught up with trying to figure out whether this outfit is the best one for you; whether all the monks are wise, enlightened people, who have any right to tell you what to do; feeling guilty because you get angry and you think you shouldn't – and all the other complex mental creations around anything that happens during the day! We weave all these complexities around things. Some monk says, "Do the dishes!" and you think, "How dare he talk to me like that. I've been meditating many more years than he has. I've written books on Buddhism. I have a degree from the University of Wisconsin, a Ph.d. in Buddhist Studies...*and that nincompoop tells me to do the dishes!*"

Don't make problems out of life's conditions, but keep recollecting. This way of recollecting, realization, is more important than trying to make everything just right...trying to straighten out all the monks and all the *anagarikas,* or trying to make Chithurst into a perfect place where you feel that everybody is exactly what they should be. It's like trying to make everything in the world perfect – just an endless, hopeless job; you cannot do it. Recognize, as long as things are adequate, use your life here for this kind of practice. Don't waste it on unnecessary complaining or fantasising, projecting all kings of things onto other beings or feeling guilty because some of your reactions and feelings aren't what you think they should be. Do you see what I mean? The important thing is not trying to think perfect thoughts or to act like saints but to realize *the way things are.* What can be realized now is whatever is going on in your mind, in your consciousness. So it's an immediate practice, here and now.

Our form is always moral, which means not to use our physical conditions, verbal abilities for harmful, cruel, selfish, exploitive activities, but to relate to each other in an active way with kindness, compassion, love – relating to each other in gentle ways. If you can't love someone, just be kind to them. If you feel a lot of hatred and anger towards me, at least refrain from hitting and killing me. That's all I ask! Practice *metta* for those you can't stand and want to kill. It's all right to have those feelings but just keep realizing them as feelings without acting on them. You are not expected to never have any unkind thoughts. So we do keep within that limitation, always within the impeccable form of *sīla.* Also we actively help each other: with *dāna,* being charitable, kindly, considerate, generous with each other, that helps us get along in a pleasant way. When we share and are kind to each other life is much more enjoyable than when we don't. It's really much nicer when people are kind and generous (at least I find it so) than when they're not. However, if you can't be kind and generous and charitable, at least refrain from being evil, doing nasty things.

Realize that everything that arises passes away and is not self. A constant refrain, isn't it? A realizing. Whatever your hang ups are, let them become fully conscious so that you begin to realize them as conditions, rather than personal problems. Let go of the identity of yourself as having problems with this or that and realize the problems we do have are conditions that come and go and change. They are not 'me', not 'mine'; they are not 'what I am'. You are continually recollecting until you begin to break through ; until, as you develop in this way, the mind begins to clear, because you are allowing things to cease. You're not reinforcing habits all the time ; you are allowing habits that have arisen to cease, to end, and you begin to find a calm, a peace - an unshakeable peace within yourself.

Ven. Ajahn Chah and Ajahn Sumedho in Hampstead

Photo : David Channer

*'It may be, Ānanda, that in some of you the thought may arise,
"The word of the master is ended, we have no teacher anymore!"
But it is not thus, Ānanda, that you should regard it. The Truths,
and the Rules of the Order, which I have set forth and laid down
for you all, let them, after I am gone, be the Teacher to you.'*

Digha Nikāya XVI — 153

ATTACHMENT TO TEACHERS

I've been asked to talk on the human problem of preference and choice*. People have many problems with preferring one monk, one teacher, or one tradition to another. They get adjusted, or attached to, a certain teacher and find that because of that they can't learn from any other teacher. This is an understandable human problem because our preferences for one allow us to be open to what he or·she is saying, and when somebody else comes along we don't want to open up and learn from them. We may not like them, or we might feel doubtful or uncertain about them, and so we tend to resent and not want to listen to them. Or, we may have heard rumours, and have opinions and views that this teacher is *this* way and that one is *that* way.

Now the structure of Buddhist convention is designed mainly to pay respect to Buddha, Dhamma and Sangha rather than to a particular personality or guru, in order to cut through this human failing of attachment to a charismatic teacher. The Sangha, as represented by the bhikkhu-sangha, is worthy of respect and worthy of alms if they live according to the Discipline; and that's a better standard than deciding whether we like them, or their personalities agree with ours. Sometimes we learn a lot from having to listen to, and obey, some particular person we may not like very much or have conflict with. Human nature is to try to adjust our lives so that we are always with or following somebody we feel especially compatible with. For example at Wat Nong Pah Pong, it was always easy to follow somebody like Ajahn Chah – because one

---

* This talk was given, and recorded, on the request of the Auckland Theravada Buddhist Association, New Zealand.

felt so much respect and admiration for such a teacher that it was no problem to go and do things, or to listen to what he said and to obey his every word. Sometimes one did feel conflict or resentment, but because of the power of such a person, one could always let go of one's pride and conceit. But, at times we were faced with having to be with bhikkhus who were senior to us who we didn't particularly like or even respect, and we could see many faults and personality traits in them that we found offensive. However, in training under the Discipline, we would do what was proper, what was appropriate and suitable, rather than just be petty and run away, or insult, or carry unpleasant thoughts in our minds towards that particular person. It was a very good training. Sometimes Ajahn Chah would, I think, deliberately send us off to be with difficult people that gave us a chance to mellow a bit, to give in a bit and to learn to do the right thing rather than just to follow the particular emotion that might be aroused at the time.

Now all of us have our own kind of personality. We can't help that, our personalities are just as they happen to be, and whether one finds them charming or boring, this isn't a matter of Dhamma but of personal preference and compatibility. The practice of the Dhamma means that we no longer seek to attach to friendship or liking someone – we are no longer seeking to be only with that which we like and esteem, but instead to be able to maintain a balance under all conditions. So our training under the Vinaya Discipline is always to do what is right through action or speech, rather than to use action and speech for what is harmful, petty, cruel, selfish or egotistical. Vinaya gives us the chance to practise under all kinds of situations and conditions.

I notice in this country people have strong attachments to various teachers. They say *"My teacher is this. He is my teacher, and I can't go to any other teacher because I'm loyal and devoted to my teacher."* This is a very English sense of devotion and loyalty to someone, to the point where it becomes too much. One becomes bound to an ideal, to a person, rather than to the truth. Our refuges are deliberately set up as Buddha, Dhamma and Sangha, rather than as the personality of any teacher. You don't take refuge in Ajahn Chah, or in any of the bhikkus here...unless you are an unusually silly person.

You could say *"Ajahn Sumedho is* **my** *teacher; Ajahn Tiradhammo is* **not** *my teacher. I'll only learn from Venerable Sucitto* and not from any other"* - along like that. We can create all kinds of problems in this way, can't we? *"I'm a Theravāda Buddhist, therefore I can't learn from those Tibetan Buddhists or those Zen Buddhists"*. It's very easy for us to become sectarian in this way, because if something is different from what we're used to, we suspect it as not being as good or as pure as what we've devoted ourselves to. But in meditation, what we are aiming at is truth, full understanding and enlightenment, inclining away from the jungle of selfishness, conceit, pride and human passions. So it's not very wise to attach to a particular teacher to the point where you refuse to learn from any other.

Now some teachers encourage this attitude. They say *"Once you take me as your teacher, then don't you go to any other teacher! Don't you learn from any other tradition! If you accept me as your teacher, you can't go to any other."* There are a lot of teachers that bind you to themselves in that way, and they have very good reasons sometimes, because people just 'go shopping'. They go from one teacher to another teacher, and another...and never learn anything. But I think the problem is not so much in 'shopping' as in attaching to a teacher, or to a tradition to the point where you have to exclude all others. That makes for a sect, a sectarian mind with which people cannot recognise wisdom or learn from anything unless it's in the exact words and conventions that they are used to. That keeps us very limited, narrow and frightened. People become afraid to listen to another teacher because it might cause doubt to arise in their minds, or they might feel that they are not being a loyal student of their particular tradition. The Buddhist path is to develop wisdom – loyalty and devotion help in that, but if they are ends in themselves, then they are obstacles.

Now 'wisdom' in this way means that we must use wisdom in our practice of meditation. How do we do that? How do we use wisdom? – *by recognising our own particular forms of pride, conceit, and the attach-*

---

* Ajahn Tiradhammo and Ven. Sucitto were the two bhikkhus next senior to Ajahn Sumedho at Chithurst when the talk was given.

ments we have to our views and opinions, to the material world, to the
tradition and the teacher, and to the friends we have. Now this doesn't
mean that we think we shouldn't attach, or that we should get rid of all
these. That's not wise either, because wisdom is the ability to observe
attachment and understand it and let go – rather than attach to ideas
that we shouldn't be attached to anything. Sometimes you hear monks
or nuns, people here saying *"Don't attach to anything."* – so we attach
to the view that we shouldn't be attached: *"I'm not going to attach to
Ajahn Sumedho, I can learn from anybody; I'm going to leave just to
prove I'm not attached to Venerable Sumedho."* So then you're attaching
to the idea that you shouldn't be attached to me, or you've got to go
away to prove that you're not attached – which isn't it at all. That's
not being wise, is it? You're just attaching to something else. You may
go to Brockwood Park and hear Krishnamurti, and then you think –
*"I'm not going to attach to those religious conventions, all that bowing,
Buddha images, monks, all that stuff. Krishnamurti says it's all pop-
pycock – 'Don't have anything to do with it, all that is useless' "* So you
attach to the view that religious conventions are all useless and you
shouldn't have anything to do with them. But that's also an attachment,
isn't it – attachment to views and opinions, and if you attach to what
Krishnamurti says, or you attach to what I say, it's still an attachment.
So we're recognising attachment, and it's wisdom that recognises attachment. This doesn't mean that we have to attach to any other opinion,
but to just recognise and know attachment frees us from being deluded
by the attachments we do make.

Now recognise that attaching does have a certain value. We have
to learn to walk first of all by crawling, just by waving our arms and
legs. If a baby is born, the mother doesn't say *"Don't wave your arms and
legs like that! Walk!"* or *"You'll always be dependent on me, nursing
at my breast, clinging to me all the time, you'll just be clinging to your
mother all your life !".* The baby needs to attach to the mother. Now if
it's the mother's intention to keep the baby attached to her all the time,
then it's not very wise of her. But when we can allow people to attach
to us in order to give them strength, so that when they have strength
they can let go of us, that 's compassion, isn't it?

Conventional forms are things that we can use according to time and place and wisely consider and learn from, rather than forming an opinion that we shouldn't be attached to anything, but be completely independent and self-sufficient. The position of a Buddhist monk is a very dependent existence. We are dependent on the requisites for existence; on food, on robes, on a place to live and medicine for illness. We have no money, no way of cooking food, growing food or providing for ourselves. We have to depend on the kindness of other people for the basic necessities of life. People say *"Why don't you grow your own food, and become self-sufficient so that you don't need all these people ? You can be independent."* That's highly valued in our society's terms, isn't it, to be self-sufficient, independent, not in debt to anyone, not dependent on anything. Yet there are these rules and conventions designed by Gotama the Buddha - they weren't designed by me. If I had my way, I would probably have designed it differently : it would be nice to be self-sufficient, have my little cabbage patch all to myself, my private funds, my little hermitage- *"I don't need you, I'm independent and free, self-sufficient"*.

When I took ordination, I didn't really know what I was getting into - I found out later that I had made myself totally and completely dependent on other people, and my family had the white, middle-class, Anglo-Saxon, self-sufficient, independent, don't-depend-on - anyone type of philosophy. We call it in America, the W.A.S.P. - White, Anglo-Saxon, Protestant - syndrome. You're not like Southern Europeans that depend on their mamas and all that. You are completely independent from your mother, and father, you're Protestant – no Popes, none of that stuff: You are not subservient. Black people might have to be in a subservient position, but being white, Anglo-Saxon, Protestant means that you're at the top of the social scale – you're the best. Then I found myself in a Buddhist country, taking samanera ordination at the age of thirty-two. In Thailand little boys ordain as samaneras, so I had to sit with the little Thai boys all the time. Here I was, six foot two, thirty-two years old, having to sit and eat my meals and fall in line with little boys – it was very embarassing for me. I had to be dependent on people to give me food, or whatever, I couldn't have any money.

So I considered this:*"What is the purpose of this? What is the value? What did the Buddha mean? Why did he do it this way? Why didn't he follow the White, Anglo - Saxon Protestant values, like my parents?"*

But I began to appreciate the need, the goodness, of being dependent in the right way, of admitting interdependence. It takes some humility, doesn't it, to learn to be dependent on others again. Now, with pride and conceit, one thinks *"I don't want to be in debt or owe anything to anybody."* And then we humbly recognise our dependence on each other here, dependence on the anagarikas *(postulants)* on the anagarikās *(nuns)* on the lay people, on the junior monks. Even though I'm senior bhikkhu here, I'm still very dependent on the rest of you. This is always to be considered in one's life, rather than to be rejected or to resent, because we recognise that we are always interdependent, helping each other – and this is a dependence based on conventions and on the material world, and on compassionate and joyous relationships. Even if we don't have any joy or love for each other, we can at least be kind, not vindictive or nasty to each other. We can trust each other.

Don't expect any social situation, any society, any organisation or group to be perfect or to be an end in itself. It's only a conventional form, and like anything, it is unsatisfactory if you're expecting to be completely satisfied through it or by it. Any teacher or guru that you attach to will inevitably disappoint you in some respect – even if they are saintly gurus, they still die...or they disrobe and marry 16 year old girls...they might do anything: The history of religious idols can be really disillusioning! I used to consider, when I was a young bhikkhu in Thailand – what would I do if Ajahn Chah suddenly said *"Buddhism is a farce! I want nothing to do with it! I'm going to disrobe and marry a rich woman."* What would I do if Ajahn Buddhadasa, one of the famous scholar-monks of Thailand, said *"Studying Buddhism all these years is a farce, it's a waste of time. I'm going to become a Christian!"* What would I do if the Dalai Lama disrobed and married an American lady? What would I do if Venerable Sucitto and Tiradhammo and all these people just suddenly said *"I'm going to leave. I want to go out and have some fun!"* If all the anagarikas suddenly said *"I'm fed up with this!"*? All the nuns ran away with the anagarikas? What would I do?

Does my being a monk depend on the support or devotion of all the other people around me, or the pronouncements of Ajahn Chah or the Dalai Lama? Does my practice of meditation depend upon support from others, encouragement, and having everybody live up to my expectations? If it does, it could easily be destroyed, couldn't it ?

When I was a junior monk, I used to consider that I must have confidence in my own insight and not depend on everyone around me supporting my particular position, and through the years I've had many chances to be disillusioned in this life...but I keep reflecting rather than depending on everything going in a positive way for me. What I'm doing I have confidence in, from my own understanding of it, not because I believe or need the support and approval of others. In your life you must ask these questions – is your becoming a samana – a monk or a nun – dependent on me encouraging you, upon the others, upon hope, expectations for the future, upon rewards and all that? Or is it determination in your own right to realise the truth? Then stay within the particular conventional form, pushing it to its ultimate just to see how far it can take you, rather than give up when it doesn't, when you begin to be disillusioned with the whole thing. I remember sometimes at Wat Pah Pong just feeling so fed up with things and feeling so negative towards the other monks, not because they did anything very wrong, but just because I became depressed and couldn't see anything other than just negative views. Then it was necessary to observe that, rather than to believe it, for one endures through the unendurable only to find that one can endure anything.

So we're not here to find *my* teacher, but to be willing to learn from everything – from the rats and the mosquitoes, from the inspired teachers, from the depressed ones, from the ones that disappoint us and the ones that' never disappoint us – because we're not trying to find perfection in conventional forms, or in teachers. Last year, I went back to Thailand and saw Tan Ajahn Chah very ill, not the same ebullient, humorous, lovable man I used to know...just like a sack of flesh sitting there like *that*...and I would think *"Oh I wish Ajahn Chah weren't like that. My teacher, Ajahn Chah is my teacher, and I don't want him to be like that. I want him to be like the Ajahn Chah I used to know, that you could sit and listen to, and then you could tell Ajahn Chah stories to all the other monks."* You'd say- *"Do you remember Ajahn Chah said this, this wonderfully wise thing that Ajahn Chah said?"* Then somebody else from another tradition says – *"Well our teacher said this."* So you have a competition as to who's the wisest. Then when *your* teacher sits there like a sack of flesh, you say – *"Ohhh...maybe I chose the wrong teacher..."* But the desire to have a teacher, the *best* teacher, the teacher that never fails you, is suffering, isn't it?

The point of the Buddhist teaching is to be able to learn from living teachers or from dead ones. When Ajahn Chah dies, we can still learn from him – go look at his corpse! You say *"I don't want Ajahn Chah to be a corpse, I want him to be the ebullient, humorous, lovable teacher I knew twenty years ago. I don't want him to be just a rotting corpse with worms coming out of his eyes."* How many of you are willing to look at your loved ones when they're dead, when you want to remember them at their best? Just like my mother now – she has a picture of me when I was 17 years old, graduated from high school, wearing a suit and tie, with my hair nicely combed – you know how they take pictures in professional studios so that you look much better than you ever really do. So this picture is hanging in my mother's room of me. Mothers want to think of their sons as always being clean cut and handsome, young... but what if I died and started rotting away, maggots coming out of my eyes, and somebody took a picture of me and sent it to my mother? It would be monstrous wouldn't it, to put it beside the picture of me when I was 17 years old! But this is like holding onto an image of Ajahn Chah as he was five years ago, and then seeing him as he is now.

As a meditator, one can use this life as we experience it by reflecting on it, learning from it, rather than demanding that teachers, sons, daughters, mothers or whatever remain in their perfect form always. We make that demand when we never really look at them, never really get to know anyone very well, just hold on to an ideal, an image that we preserve and never question or learn from. For a meditator, everything is teaching us something...if we're willing to learn to coexist with it, with the successes and failures, the living and the dead, the good memories and the disappointments. And what do we learn? - *that these are only conditions of our mind.* They're the things that we create and attach to - and whatever we attach to is going to take us to despair and death. That's the ending of whatever begins. So we learn from that. We learn from our sorrows and grief, our disillusionment, and we can let go, we can allow life to operate following the laws of Nature and witness this, freeing ourselves from the illusion of self as being connected with the mortal condition. And so all conditions take us to the unconditioned - even our sorrow and grief take us to emptiness, freedom and liberation, if we are humble and patient.

Sometimes life is easier when we don't have too many choices to make. When you have too many wonderful gurus all the time it must be a bit frustrating, to have to listen to so much fantastic wisdom bubbling out from so many charismatic, wise sages. But even the wisest sages, the finest human beings in the world today, are only conditions of our mind. The Dalai Lama, Ajahn Chah, Buddhadāsa, Tan Chao Khun Paññānanda,* the Pope, Archbishop of Canterbury, Margaret Thatcher, and Mr. Reagan...are nothing but conditions of our own mind, aren't they? We have likes, dislikes and prejudices, but these are things conditioned into the mind - and all these conditions, hatred or love or whatever, take us to the unconditioned if we are patient and enduring and willing to use wisdom. You might find it easier to believe what *I* say, it's easier than finding out for yourself, but believing what I say is not going to nourish *you.* The wisdom that I use in my life is nourishing me only. It might encourage you to *use* wisdom, but you have to actually eat the food yourself to be nourished, rather than believe what I say. The Buddhist path is just that - a way for each one of us to realise the truth - it throws us back onto ourselves again, making us look and reflect on our lives rather than being caught in the devotion and hope that take us to their opposites.

So consider what I've said this evening and reflect on it. Don't believe it, don't disbelieve it. If you have any prejudices or opinions and views, it's allright, just see them as they are, as conditions of your mind, and learn from them.

---

* A highly-respected Thai bhikkhu who was staying at Chithurst at the time.